Faithful to Our Tasks

Faithful to Our Tasks

Arkansas's Women and the Great War

Elizabeth Griffin Hill

Little Rock, Arkansas

The Butler Center for Arkansas Studies
Central Arkansas Library System
100 Rock Street
Little Rock, Arkansas 72201

www.butlercenter.org

First edition: March 2017
ISBN 978-1-945624-00-1

Manager: Rod Lorenzen
Book design: Mike Keckhaver
Cover design: H. K. Stewart
Copyeditor: Ali Welky

Library of Congress Cataloging-in-Publication Data

Names: Hill, Elizabeth Griffin, author.
Title: Faithful to our tasks: Arkansas's women and the Great War /
by Elizabeth Griffin Hill.
Description: First edition. | Little Rock, Arkansas : Butler Center Books, a division of the Butler Center for Arkansas Studies at the Central Arkansas Library System, [2017] | Includes bibliographical references and index.
Identifiers: LCCN 2016041642 | ISBN 9781945624001 (pbk. : alk. paper)
Subjects: LCSH: Women--Arkansas--History--20th century. | World War, 1914-1918--Women--Arkansas.
Classification: LCC F411 .H64 2017 | DDC 305.409767/0904--dc23 LC record available at https://lccn.loc.gov/2016041642

Butler Center Books, the publishing division of the Butler Center for Arkansas Studies, was made possible by the generosity of Dora Johnson Ragsdale and John G. Ragsdale Jr.

Printed in the United States of America

This book is printed on archival-quality paper that meets requirements of the American National Standard for Information Sciences, Permanence of Paper, Printed Library Materials, ANSI Z39.48-1984.

In Memoriam

Faithful to Our Tasks is dedicated to the memory of "mothers who had been in suspense for weeks and months, not knowing where their boys were located, [who] worked, sorrowful in heart, but patriotic in spirit, doing their part." The Arkansas mothers were described as faithful workers in the Red Cross workrooms, who sacrificed and saved and did without necessities in order that their sons fighting in Europe might be cared for. The book is also dedicated to Arkansas's women who labored on the front lines as nurses and Red Cross workers, and to their mothers, who remained at home.

(The above quote is from the Report of the Arkansas Woman's Committee, 72. Mrs. Frank Peel, chairman of publicity, paid homage to the "loyal churchwomen of Arkansas" as an organized group. However, her words are appropriate to honor all mothers who labored in Red Cross workrooms across Arkansas as their sons and daughters were in harm's way.)

Table of Contents

Acknowledgements

As I contemplate the journey that culminated in *Faithful to Our Tasks*, my first thoughts are of Guy Lancaster and Michael Polston, who invited me to write about Arkansas's women during the Great War in their enlightening anthology, *To Can the Kaiser*, published by Butler Center Books in 2015. I was honored to be included among some of Arkansas's premier scholars. Later, both Lancaster and Polston encouraged me to expand my extensive primary research into a book solely about Arkansas's women during the war. I also want to acknowledge the assistance from archivists and archival assistants at the University of Arkansas at Little Rock's Center for Arkansas History and Culture, the Butler Center for Arkansas Studies of the Central Arkansas Library System, Special Collections at the University of Arkansas in Fayetteville, and the Arkansas State Archives.

I so appreciate Rod Lorenzen, manager of Butler Center Books, who called me one Monday morning to tell me that Butler Center Books wanted to publish *Faithful to Our Tasks*. I am greatly indebted to Ali Welky, who edited my manuscript and offered invaluable suggestions. H. K. Stewart created a beautiful cover that brought tears to my eyes, and Michael Keckhaver meticulously designed the pages of the book. I am grateful to each one.

As Richard, my husband and fellow researcher, and I visited the archives at Ouachita Baptist University in Arkadelphia, Wendy Richter greeted us with records ready for our perusal. I enjoyed visiting with Raymond Screws of the Arkansas National Guard Museum at Camp Robinson and, more recently, with Stephan McAteer of the MacArthur Museum of Military History and with Cary Bradburn of the North Little Rock History Commission. Each one shared from his collection of digital photographs or propaganda posters.

I received sage advice from Thomas W. Goldstein, who reviewed *To Can the Kaiser* in a recent issue of *The Arkansas Historical Quar-*

terly (vol. 74, no. 3, 2015). Goldstein described my essay as well documented and fascinating; however, he was disappointed that I did not go further and show how Arkansas women's actions during the war fit into the big picture of women's history. As a result, I have done extensive secondary research to complement my archival findings, and I now anticipate that *Faithful to Our Tasks* will make a significant contribution to the scholarship on the subject.

Introduction: "Faithful to Our Tasks"[1]

Primary records of the World War I era, discovered in archives around central Arkansas, revealed that the state's women were suddenly faced with a devastating world war for which they were expected to make a significant contribution of time and effort. Organized or "club" women were already tackling myriad problems to be found in abundance within Arkansas—a poor, rural state—as they worked for better schools, a centralized education system, children's well-being, and improved medical care. However, under wartime conditions, their contributions were magnified. The women followed a barrage of directions from Washington within a disconcerting display of micro-management by the federal government. The important take-away, however, is that the Great War prompted Arkansas's organized women—as well as women throughout the nation—to step forward and excel, causing men and governments to take notice.

In addition to the stereotypical bandage rolling, knitting, and cooking amid shortages, Arkansas's women were asked to tackle problems of school truancy and devastating rates of infant mortality; enlist other women in food conservation and willingness-to-serve campaigns; assist young women who poured into its major cantonment city; and oversee working women as they experienced wartime employment conditions. Notably, Arkansas's organized women were already equipped to tackle each assignment because they had been working together for several decades for the betterment of their communities under the aegis of the Arkansas Federation of Women's Clubs (AFWC). In addition to the AFWC, the Federation of Colored Women's Clubs in Arkansas was a strong organization with direct access to the governor's office.[2]

As historian Page Smith noted, "Reprehensible as were the suppression of dissent and the official and unofficial persecution of anyone who dared criticize the government, it is indisputably the case that the declaration of war triggered a mobilization of men and war materiel that astonished the world."[3] Under the leadership of President Woodrow Wilson—who had been elected on a platform of keeping America out of the war—the Council of National Defense, along with its pyramid of agencies down to the county level within each state, was able to carry on its work in support of its military, America's allies, and the numerous requirements of those remaining at home. Although today's citizen would likely find the federal government's control over volunteer men and women's activities alarming, such power allowed the government to standardize contributions, eliminate duplication of efforts, and raise millions of dollars to fund the military.

One hundred years ago, when America entered the Great War on April 6, 1917, the United States was not prepared to provide an army of four million men with adequate warm clothing to survive European winters. Added to the requirements of our own military were the needs of our European allies, who had been fighting for three years and were on the brink of starvation without our help. To whom could the U.S. government turn but its citizens? And to whom but its women could it turn for warm clothing and food conservation? Although nowadays a woman might serve the cause by enlisting in the military itself, many women today would have difficulty comprehending the extent to which the government depended on its citizens to accept roles that would now be filled by manufacturers or social service agencies.

The Great War also intensified changes for working women, most of whom were young and single, as they were thrust into traditionally male-oriented jobs. They were forced to deal with men who resented their willingness to work for less pay, and they came to realize that as women in other parts of the country entered unionized factory positions, salary disparities increased among women workers in various regions of the country. And shortages caused by the war provided opportunities for women to increase their presence in such fields as teaching and the higher echelons of clerical work. Although women were the only members of the newly recognized nursing profession, they earned long-sought respect during the war as shortages made the profession invaluable. Added to the mix was a suffrage campaign that intensified as men noticed women's significant contributions to the war effort.

During the war, however, most of Arkansas's suffragists refused to identify with the militant group of women who made the daily newspapers as they picketed the White House. Arkansas's women had mixed reactions to the suffrage movement. Even the AFWC did not embrace it until 1915. Women in rural areas especially expressed concern about the movement, refusing to register for food conservation or willingness-to-serve campaigns because they feared being forced to vote if they signed their names to a government paper. In the Report of the Woman's Committee, Council of Defense for Arkansas[4] (the "Arkansas Woman's Committee"), the women's suffrage organizations in Arkansas noted that members had set aside most of their suffrage activities as they worked for the Red Cross and the Arkansas Woman's Committee.[5]

This report focuses on the eighteen months in which the United States was a vital participant in the Great War. However, this time was only a brief part of an era of change for women as they moved out of the Victorian nineteenth century and came into their own as social activists during the early years of the twentieth century. Additional research into secondary sources provides context for what influenced women's actions and reactions during the war. The report incorporates the mitigating factors and experiences of American women in general and compares Arkansas women's Progressive Era actions with those of other southern women. The contextual underpinnings provide a rich tapestry as we attempt to understand our grandmothers' and great-grandmothers' responses to wartime needs.

As an example of what was important to women of the era, in January 1917, Governor Charles H. Brough, whose wife, Anne, was a high-profile activist within the state, assured suffragists that he would do all that he could to ensure women's right to vote in state elections because women should have a say in "all questions affecting property, education, and morality."[6] And women were satisfied with those narrow parameters. In addition, as the 1917 state legislative session came to a close, women rejoiced in their victories, which included a bill authorizing women's suffrage in state primaries; bills providing for a board of charities and correction and for mothers' pensions; appropriations for boys' and girls' industrial schools and for state aid to high schools; and bills dealing with child labor and juvenile courts.[7]

In her primary research of Arkansas's club women at the turn of the century, Frances Mitchell Ross found that "although the New Woman belonged to the Progressive Era of the twentieth century, she was a product of the nineteenth century."[8] Ross noted, however, that the New Woman of the early twentieth century "justified an expanded role for herself, which contributed to the growth of female autonomy."[9] Ross's findings about the Progressive Era in general were verified by Arkansas's organized women during the Great War, whose noteworthy contributions, combined with those of women all over the United States, culminated in a change of attitude toward women, perhaps only briefly.

Although Arkansas's middle-class club women took the reins and led the way in the war work on the homefront, it should be noted that women of all classes and races signed registration cards during a February 1918 statewide campaign to ascertain women's willingness and availability to work in various civilian jobs. The state's non-elite women also worked within their own homes to "starve the garbage pail" and to knit and sew for "the boys" in the trenches of France. In its final report, which was incorporated into the Report of the Arkansas Woman's Committee in December 1918, the Crawford County Woman's Committee noted that in Van Buren, 736 white women and fifty-three African American women completed registration-for-service cards during the campaign. Two registrants—Julia Wade, a young African American woman, and Astelle Norfleet, a young working-class white woman—are featured in chapter seven, "Registering Women for Service"; their cards are in the photographs section. African American ministers were active in communicating wartime needs to their congregations, and women leaders were trained to work on various projects within their own communities. County committees' references to contributions or actions by African American women are included within applicable chapters.[10]

Chapter 1: Organizing the Arkansas Woman's Committee

"The Woman's Committee is concerned, through its different departments, [with] safeguarding the moral and spiritual forces of the nation so that those inner defenses of our national life may not be broken down in the period of the war."[11]

Although for three years the United States had refrained from entering the Great War, which began in Europe in 1914, Congress created the Council of National Defense[12] as a part of the Army Appropriation Act, approved on August 29, 1916. The council, which was charged with the "co-ordination of industries and resources for the national security and welfare" and with the "creation of relations which will render possible in time of need the immediate concentration and utilization of the resources of the Nation,"[13] was composed of members of the president's cabinet, with Secretary of War Newton D. Baker as chairman. Other members were the Secretaries of the Navy, the Interior, Agriculture, Commerce, and Labor. President Woodrow Wilson appointed the Advisory Commission, made up of seven distinguished citizens who were well known in the fields of business, labor, and science.[14]

Soon after war was declared, the Council of National Defense called upon President Wilson to authorize the organization of state councils, which would be tasked with assisting the national council in carrying out its purposes. At President Wilson's behest, Governor Charles H. Brough appointed twelve men to serve as the Council of Defense for Arkansas, which held its first meeting on May 22, 1917. As the work grew and a need arose for additional members, the governor appointed twenty more men and one woman, Ida Frauenthal of Conway.[15]

On April 21, 1917, the Council of National Defense appointed the Woman's Committee, Council of National Defense (the "National Woman's Committee").[16] But a question soon emerged: With the American Red Cross already in place, why was there a need for the

National Woman's Committee? The answer could be found in acknowledging that the Red Cross had been assigned definite duties with clearly defined limits. The Red Cross was charged with helping to provide the troops with comforts and necessities while in the field, helping them in transit, and assisting the U.S. Army Medical Corps in the care of the sick and wounded. The Red Cross was also authorized to raise funds to carry on relief work for families of mobilized soldiers and sailors, and to conduct classes in first aid to the injured, elementary hygiene, home care of the sick, dietetics, and surgical dressings. The Red Cross also organized needed relief in the event of flood, famine, or pestilence.[17]

On the other hand, with responsibilities completely outside the defined parameters of the American Red Cross, the National Woman's Committee was tasked with registration of women for general service; food production and conservation; oversight of industrial conditions concerning women and children; child education and welfare; education of women along all lines outside of the Red Cross service; and maintenance of all existing social agencies. The overriding purpose of the National Woman's Committee was "safeguarding the moral and spiritual forces of the nation so that those inner defenses of our national life may not be broken down in the period of the war."[18]

Following organization of the National Woman's Committee, the next step was for states to organize their own woman's councils. On July 1, Governor Charles H. Brough appointed the Woman's Committee, Council of Defense for Arkansas (the "Arkansas Woman's Committee"), with his wife, Anne Brough, as honorary chairman and Ida Frauenthal as temporary chairman. Eventually, other members of the committee's executive committee were appointed, including six officers and sixteen departmental chairmen. Frauenthal became permanent chairman and received her appointment as the only woman member of the Council of Defense for Arkansas as well. The National Woman's Committee's chairmen were responsible for departments of legislation, child welfare, registration, food administration, home economics, health and recreation, home and foreign relief, maintenance of existing social service agencies, women in industry, education, the speaker's bureau, Liberty Loan, War Savings Stamps, publicity, training for service, and Americanization. Although some departments were not fully developed in Arkansas, several had extensive responsibilities.[19]

Chapter 2: Registering Women to Conserve

"Belgian babies are carefully examined to see if they can live with-out being fed today, while our relief workers feed those who were not fed the day before, and that without a campaign of education to the situation, we may continue to waste our crumbs."[20]

During the tumultuous summer of 1917—as the United States went into full-combat mode and conservation plans were in pro-cess—the Arkansas Woman's Committee received its first orders. As the newly appointed committee planned to meet for the first time on July 2, a letter, dated June 22,[21] arrived from the National Woman's Committee. The letter laid out the state committee's role in a food conservation campaign—to begin July 1. The short timeframe was caused by an unintentional leak to the press in Washington, thus re-quiring state committees to get the campaign underway despite their lack of time to prepare. A portion of the letter provided insight into the national food situation during the summer of 1917 as well as an early glimpse into the federal government's methods of maintaining control over states' activities: "It is literally true that there will not be enough food in the world to maintain the population if present methods are followed. Founded upon this fact, the program for food conservation is briefly stated as follows:

1st	An exact survey of the amount of food on hand in this country, so that the amount available for home consumption and exportation to the allies may be accurately known.
2nd	An investigation undertaken by the Department of Agriculture into the normal consumption of food by different families from representative groups of the population.
3rd	Some control of food in storage, better methods of transportation, and the elimination of speculation in foodstuffs.
4th	The enrollment of a league of women who will pledge themselves to carry out the wishes of the President, the National Government, and the Food Administration.

The last part of the program will be the first to be put into oper-ation, and from July 1st to July 15th an intensive campaign will be undertaken through every possible medium of publicity. This is intended to create such a sentiment in favor of the Food Administration program that women throughout the country will gladly sign the pledge cards and promise to carry out the instructions of the Food Administration."[22]

The letter continued, noting that "since this matter chiefly concerns women, it is clear that leadership must in a large measure be given over to the women themselves."[23] The letter also stressed that the entire woman's committee of each state must work together on the food pledge campaign, even as it acknowledged that there likely had not been time to appoint a chairman of food conservation.[24]

An article on the "Arkansas Federation of Women's Clubs" (AFWC) page of the Sunday, June 24, *Arkansas Gazette* announced a request for the leadership of all women's societies throughout the state to attend an organizational meeting at the Hotel Marion in Little Rock on Monday, July 2. The twenty-five women in attendance learned of the impending campaign to register housewives for food conservation. Arkansas's goal was to send 250,000 signed cards to Herbert Hoover, National Food Administrator. Women who signed the cards would thus pledge to follow the federal government's conservation guidelines. As the one-day meeting continued, the women elected six permanent officers and the chairmen of three of the sixteen departments: education, welfare of women and children, and registration. Selection of other department chairmen was deferred to the executive committee.[25]

The newly elected officers of the Arkansas Woman's Committee prepared a newspaper article, published on Sunday, July 13, that explained the purpose and functions of the committee and the mechanics of the statewide food pledge drive. The article included the name of each woman chosen to be her county's committee chairman; the woman whose name was listed was to then assume the chairmanship. Although letters were sent to most of the selectees, the list provided notification for those who had not received a letter. Any chairman who was unable to serve was advised to find someone to take her place. The July 13 article also addressed the need for food conservation:

> Only a few reasons for this may be given: That we are to be called upon to feed the greater part of the world, and that at a time when something like one-fifth of our workers will be called into army camps and into industries that supply war materials, such as munitions and war vessels of all kinds; that the allies have food enough to last until September, only; that a soldier fed in France, means one less American soldier sent to France; that Belgian babies are carefully examined to see if they can live without being fed today, while our relief workers feed those who were not fed the day before, and that without a campaign of education to the situation, we may continue to waste our crumbs.[26]

The article continued by noting that women who signed the food registration card could also sign a registration-for-service card. Although neither registration was compulsory, women were certainly a part of the resources that the federal government had to mobilize for service "if the victory is won for civilization in this war."[27]

Counties had been organized with township chairmen throughout rural areas and ward chairmen throughout cities. Sign-up day was set for Saturday, July 28; however, the cards did not arrive until the next day. With insufficient time for thorough communication—and late-arriving cards—only 3,582 women signed the cards despite the original goal of 250,000 signatures. Women gave various reasons for not signing. Complaints of insufficient information topped the list of reasons not to sign, and other excuses included lack of interest; belief that one could economize without signing; fear that the government would take the family's own canned goods; and, finally, concern that families would be forced to eat corn bread.[28]

In an August 16 letter to Wallace Townsend, chairman of the Council of Defense for Arkansas, Frauenthal evaluated the campaign: "We are working hard with the Hoover cards but it is uphill work as there seems to be a decided objection to 'signing anything' and most of the women say that their husbands have cautioned them against putting their names to any sort of paper."[29] For many Arkansas women, the government's request for them to sign a pledge card simply did not sit well. Women voiced resentment of the government's interference in families' daily lives. According to the National Woman's Committee, however, the signed cards would be retained in the local area by its own woman's committee and would be available to assist the government in meeting emergencies.[30] Despite noted negative responses, a newspaper article on September 9 reported that many African American women in Jefferson County had enlisted in the food conservation campaign by "signing the Hoover food conservation cards."[31] Ten days later, another article noted that Chicot County had sent 258 signed conservation cards to the woman's committee's headquarters in Little Rock. Fifty of the signees were African American women.[32]

The late receipt of the food registration cards pointed to another fact of life four months after the United States entered the war. Minnie Rutherford-Fuller, secretary of the Arkansas Woman's Committee, noted that this was "but a very small illustration of the general upsetting of ordinary railroad and express matters, as a part of all living, which even the preparations for a war occasion. Letters which formerly came to me in 12 days, since the war require full 30 days in transit."[33] With factors such as a hurried start date decreed by Washington DC, registration cards that were not received in time, and an uninformed, wary public, the drive was surely headed for failure from the beginning.

By mid-September, plans were already being made for a second food conservation pledge drive throughout the United States. For this drive, Hamp Williams, state food administrator, appointed an executive board to oversee the work. Emma Archer, chairman of home economics and food conservation of the Arkansas Woman's Committee, was named as a member. Williams noted that the board's goal would be to reach every one of Arkansas's 365,000 families.

During the weekly meeting of the Arkansas Woman's Committee at the Board of Commerce building in Little Rock, Williams led a discussion of problems confronted during the first drive; the lack of communication and trust—particularly among the state's men— would be addressed as the second drive began.[34]

By early October, plans were distributed for church and fraternal orders to cooperate during National Pledge Card Campaign Week, set for Sunday, October 21, through Sunday, October 28. Every minister in Arkansas was asked to speak on the need for food conservation during the Sunday morning service on October 21. African American clergymen and other delegates had recently attended an agricultural and food conservation congress at Shorter College. Attendees were urged to encourage others to support food conservation as well as Red Cross work and the sale of Liberty Bonds.[35] Monsignor Thomas V. Tobin of the Catholic Church confirmed that he would see that every priest in Arkansas received a copy of the letter. Williams wrote to each of Arkansas's 640 Masonic lodges, asking for their support. The Knights of Pythias sent out letters to its 320 lodges, and the Ancient Order of United Workmen, 128 letters. Governor Brough issued a proclamation asking for the support of all citizens. Brough noted that Arkansans must be educated as to why the United States was in the war and to the necessity of each citizen's participation in food conservation. Nationally, Herbert Hoover welcomed the so-called "war mothers,"[36] i.e., women whose sons were in military service, to the ranks of women who would conduct door-to-door canvassing during the campaign.[37]

By October 24, the campaign dates had been delayed to October 28 through November 4, and every county clerk had received the county's pledge cards. Williams noted that responsibility for distribution lay with chairmen of the county Council of Defense and the county woman's committee, respectively. The cards were to receive distribution "in the schools, churches, clubs, lodges and wherever loyal and patriotic men and women are represented."[38] Williams continued, "The signing of a pledge card is merely going on record that the family represented is doing its 'bit' for the government during the war. The family which signs a pledge card will receive a beautiful window card."[39]

By Friday, October 26, signed cards were being returned at the rate of 400 to 500 daily.[40] In one final pep talk, Williams noted that he was representing the U.S. government in an appeal in which he reminded Arkansans that food would win the war. The United States had to make up for the shortages in Europe, so each Arkansan would be asked to make a sacrifice in food that would hardly be noticed. Williams compared that small sacrifice to the sacrifices made by Europe, where forty million men had been diverted from their regular occupations to war or war work and where millions of women had taken the place of husband or brother. Williams continued:

> The European harvest fields this autumn will fall 500,000,000 bushels of grain short of their normal production. Add to this the toll of the deadly submarine. Europe is 33 per cent, or 2,300,000 tons less, in its beet sugar crop than in 1915–16. The allies have killed 33,000,000 head of their stock animals.[41]

Williams's rhetoric then turned to the possibility that Germany might win the war through an undersea campaign and force England to surrender:

> Germany then could and would come to America. This country would then enter into the bloodiest and most destructive war in its history. Such a war would cost us 10 men for every one under the present circumstances and subject us to untold horrors and sacrifices, such as we cannot now conceive. If Germany wins she will colonize the world, subject it to her autocratic military rule and force heavy taxation.[42]

The AFWC page of the same newspaper reported that the Arkansas Woman's Committee had been asked to assist in the second campaign for food conservation pledges. Although Williams indicated that all family members would be asked to sign, the article quoted the pledge card, which stated, "The food administration wishes to have as members all of those actually handling food in the homes. Those signing pledges are entitled to membership window cards which will be delivered upon receipt of the signed pledge card."[43] Thus, the card clarified any question as to whether women were the prime targets of the campaign. Those who signed the pledge would also receive "a home card to hang in the kitchen, with general instructions on the conservation of bread, cereals, meat, milk, fats and fuel, and why we must send the allies more wheat, meat, butter, milk and sugar."[44]

The author of the AFWC page article—whose initials were C. E. W.[45]—shared with women her personal understanding of the reasons for the drive and the need for conservation. First, she noted that the second drive was necessary because the first drive's results were "not completely satisfactory."[46] She noted that some women felt that the government was constantly placing something under their noses to sign. But why was there a need for a pledge drive at all? She had determined the following:

> Our country has been wasteful and extravagant in the extreme. Luxuries had become necessities. There was an overabundance of many things and seemed to be no real necessity for rigid economy. Of course we had the poor ever with us, but the majority of American people were in more than comfortable circumstances. Both men and women drifted into extravagant and wasteful habits.[47]

Thus, the purpose of the pledge cards was to impress upon women the importance of their contribution to the war effort and to encourage them to treat it as an ongoing, consistently important duty.[48]

On October 31, word reached Williams that German propagandists were making every effort to discourage the signing of the food pledge cards. An earlier report had indicated that pro-German operatives were telling women throughout the country that the government was asking them to list their foodstuffs in order to confiscate them later. By November 7, however, 17,000 signed pledge cards had been received from throughout Arkansas. By November 9, Williams had sent a letter to counties, asking that the work continue until every citizen had been given the opportunity to understand and sign a pledge card. Williams asked county chairmen to submit reports showing the number of families in the county, number of cards signed, number of cards distributed, and the reason more cards were not signed. Williams indicated that those who refused to sign even after having the matter explained to them would be considered disloyal and unpatriotic. Among those, "we expect to find the traitors."[49]

Women who signed the registration card received through the mail a card with the federal government's recommendations for food conservation:

One wheatless meal a day.	Use corn, oatmeal, rye or barley bread and non-wheat breakfast foods. Cut the loaf on the table and only as required. Eat less cake and pastry.
Beef, mutton or pork not more than once daily.	Use freely vegetables and fish. At the meat meal serve smaller portions and stew instead of steaks. Make dishes of all leftover food.
Conserve the milk.	The children must have milk. Use buttermilk and sour milk for cooking and making cottage cheese. Use less cream.
Save the fats.	Use butter on the table, but not in cooking. Reduce use of fried foods.
Use less candy and sweet drinks[.]	But do not stint [on] sugar in putting up fruit and jams, they will save butter.
Save the fuel.	Use wood when you can get it.
	As a nation we eat too little greenstuffs. Double their use and improve your health. Store potatoes and other roots properly and they will keep. Begin now to can or dry all surplus garden products.
General rules	Buy less, serve smaller portions, preach the clean plate; don't eat a fourth meal; don't limit the plain food of growing children; watch out for the wastes in the community; full garbage pails in America mean empty dinner pails in America and Europe.[50]

In its final report to Washington, covering events through December 30, 1918, the Arkansas Woman's Committee was able to report that 55,000 Arkansas women had signed the food conservation cards. Although it was deemed necessary for Williams to take over the campaign, using scathing rhetoric in order to demand the support of husbands in the conservation drive, the women would have one more opportunity to conduct a successful drive.[51]

Chapter 3: Making Do in the Kitchen (1917)

"Stone County 'stood behind the guns' when it came to food con-servation and food production. Everyone planted larger gardens, and raised more chickens and hogs."[52]

As the United States came closer to entering the war, conser-vation was regularly a topic in daily newspapers. Food prices had increased by 19 percent during the year ending January 15, 1917. The 10 percent price increase for pork chops, however, gave no in-dication of the scarcity of meat soon to be the norm. The 38 percent rise in the price of wheat flour, on the other hand, forecast its upcom-ing status as one of wartime Arkansas's scarcest commodities. Sug-ar—of which there was a distressing shortage toward the end of the war—was not yet of concern in spring 1917.[53]

Since Arkansas's housewives were primarily responsible for the family dinner table, their cooperation was vital to any statewide con-servation efforts. During March 1917—as the spring and summer growing season was emerging—the thrift garden movement made its way across the country. Union Trust Company, however, purchased a newspaper advertisement that discouraged the planting of a home garden. The ad noted that most home gardens cost more than pur-chasing individual vegetables because "women don't know how to do it"[54] and use too much fertilizer. Continuing, the ad argued that the result of women's labor would be "the usual spurt in the spring in the production of a few radishes and onions, scraggly lettuce, etc., [which] is hardly worth while."[55]

Despite Union Trust's obvious lack of faith in women's thrift gardens, the home demonstration agents of the barely three-year-old Cooperative Extension Service—along with public-school domes-tic-science teachers—began training women in safe and appropri-ate canning techniques. The stated objective was to instruct house-wives to can the produce from home gardens. Although the home demonstration work was established by the federal Smith-Lever Act of 1914 to aid rural women in making life better for their families, during the war the agents provided vital information for women who lived in cities and towns as well. Newspaper columns—laden with home economists' advice, menus, and recipes—rotated their emphasis routinely as one month's commodity shortage gave way to the next month's featured concern.

In June, Gertrude Lane, editor of the *Woman's Home Companion* magazine, launched a nationwide campaign against food waste, noting that, although women were "loyally patriotic,"[56] they must be practical and reasonable and understand that they could not leave their husbands and children to become war nurses or wireless operators. Instead, they could eliminate the garbage pail by being frugal in preparing meals for their families and by using leftovers. As women economized in such mundane ways, they would contribute a great service to the nation. Arkansas's women would be reminded throughout the war of the importance of such practical, unimaginative contributions.[57]

Conservation of manpower was imperative as well. On July 10, in response to a request from the Commercial Economy Board of the Council of National Defense, Little Rock master bakers pledged not to accept returns of unsold bread. Although a portion of the returned bread was normally sold at a reduced rate to charitable institutions and the poor, the board found that by eliminating the cost of carrying the bread to and from retailers, bakers could afford to sell the same amount of bread to charity at a reduced rate. The bakers appealed to housewives to cooperate by placing their bread orders a day in advance. The bakers noted, "We trust that we may have a prompt demonstration from the housewives of Little Rock of their desire to serve our country in this a grave national necessity."[58]

At about the same time, the Commercial Economy Board also launched a nationwide campaign that targeted "the popular American prejudice against 'totin' bundles in public.'"[59] With a Washington DC, June 30, dateline, the newspaper article announced its campaign. "A heavy drain on the country's economic resources is caused yearly, says the committee[,] by the person who insists that his tooth brush or cake of toilet soap be rushed to his home in a truck manned by two men, whose services otherwise might have been utilized in a military capacity by the government."[60] Throughout August, the AFWC page of the *Arkansas Gazette* ran articles on the subject on three successive Sundays, with subtitles such as "Women can render great service to government by assisting merchants in eliminating needless expense,"[61] as well as, "But give us a discount, say Washington women."[62] The nationwide campaign was launched in July 1917, but the practice did not go away quietly. During the following Christmas season, Stifft's Jewelers in Little Rock placed a small insert at the top of its newspaper ads, encouraging customers to carry their own packages. The jeweler pledged to give one cent to the Red Cross for every package the customer carried home. By July 1918—eleven months after the initial pronouncement—an M. M. Cohn department store advertisement included a small square in the upper right-hand corner: "One delivery a day by request of the government."[63]

Although the Arkansas Woman's Committee was tasked with overall coordination of food conservation, its officers continued to turn to the home demonstration program of the Cooperative Extension Service for the day-to-day education of the state's women. With the Secretary of Agriculture serving on the Council of National Defense, the Department of Agriculture played a vital role in both food production and conservation. The fledgling Cooperative Extension Service—a collaboration between state land-grant colleges and the U.S. Department of Agriculture—was officially created by Congress through the Smith-Lever Act of 1914, with funding provided equally among three separate entities: county, state, and federal governments. In Arkansas, home demonstration activities for women under the Smith-Lever Act began in 1915 with only seven counties taking up the work.[64]

During the war years, however, the program expanded as Connie J. Bonslagel, chair of the Arkansas Woman's Committee's department of food production and home economics, joined county woman's committee chairmen in lobbying the levying boards to provide funding for county agents. Bonslagel, who served as state home demonstration agent from 1917 until May 1950, reported that the home demonstration force increased during the summer[65] to 113 agents, twenty-nine of whom were African American.[66] Several of the agents, including at least two in urban areas, were hired temporarily for the war emergency. The estimated value of food produced by home demonstration members' home gardens, flocks of chickens, and family cows was $500,000. In less than three months' time, 1,003 women produced 18,000 pounds of cottage cheese. In Crawford County alone, 700 women raised an average of 100 fall chickens each. These efforts freed up carloads of smoked meats for shipment to Europe.[67]

Just as the second food conservation campaign was in full swing, wheat became the first major commodity shortage with which Arkansas's women had to contend. With 55,000 women signing the government's food conservation cards, it was necessary to provide them with recipes and menus. On October 31, 1917, Myrtle Wilson, instructor of domestic science at Little Rock High School, lectured on conserving wheat before the Housewives' League of Pulaski County. Wilson stressed that some of the substitutes were more expensive than wheat; however, economy was not the issue. She emphasized that Herbert Hoover, U.S. Food Administrator, had assured the nation that by substituting other products for one-fourth of the nation's wheat consumption, the United States would be able to provide sufficient wheat for our allies. Thus, all bread recipes incorporated substitutes for one-fourth to one-half the usual wheat flour. Participants were given samples of yeast bread, muffins, biscuits, and cookies made from soybean meal, sweet potatoes, oatmeal, rice, and rye. Wilson called for no shortening in the bread recipes since requirements for bread making were only yeast, flour, liquid, and salt. However, she noted that milk, sugar, and fat could be added. Wilson shared recipes published by the U.S. Department of Agriculture, all of which indicated neither baking time nor temperature setting.[68]

Late September brought a temporary sugar shortage. Hoover asked the American people to reduce sugar consumption so that the United States could honor France's appeal for 100,000 tons during October, likely followed by more at a later time. Hoover explained that at the time of the request, the United States had just enough sugar to meet its own needs until January 1, at which time the new West Indian crop would be available. Hoover asked that Americans reduce their consumption of candy and sugar by one-third. The reduction did not include sugar used to preserve fruits because preserves and jellies would reduce the amount of butter required for breads. On October 1, the entire American sugar industry was placed under the federal government's control. A licensing system went into effect to control the manufacture, refining, and importing of sugar. President Wilson approved this measure in order to prevent speculative prices and to ensure equitable distribution. Although temporary sugar shortages occurred in various parts of the United States, a sustained shortfall did not materialize until the second half of 1918.[69]

Toward late fall, Hoover appealed to every household, restaurant, and hotel to substitute chicken and eggs for red meat. He noted that our soldiers and allies required more meat than ever before. In order to accomplish this, he asked poultry producers to increase production. In particular, he encouraged them to save on feed by culling their flocks of non-producing hens. In January, Arkansas's home economists went a step further by encouraging city dwellers to raise chickens in their back yards. Protein comparisons found that a serving of chicken, with 21.5 percent protein, compared favorably with a porterhouse steak, with its 21.9 percent. As the situation worsened, the appeal to restaurants and hotels to make substitutions turned into official orders, which were not accepted favorably by patrons.[70]

In early November, Hamp Williams designated Tuesday of each week as a meatless day, followed by a wheatless Wednesday. Williams's declaration affected restaurants and hotels only. Boarding houses and private homes were exempted. Proprietors of eating establishments in Little Rock reported that—although most displayed conspicuous notices regarding the meatless or wheatless day—only about one in fifty patrons observed the change. A spokesman for the hotels and restaurants noted that after the first week, the names of patrons who refused to participate would be made public. A month later, boarding houses were included along with hotels and restaurants, and one wheatless meal each week was added. The shortages did not let up, and on January 17, 1918, a new conservation schedule was published for restaurants, hotels, and boarding houses:[71]

Sunday	Monday	Tuesday	Wednesday	Thursday	Friday	Saturday
		Meatless day all day	Wheatless day all day			Porkless day all day
Meatless breakfast	Meatless breakfast		Meatless breakfast	Meatless breakfast	Meatless breakfast	Meatless breakfast
Wheatless supper	Wheatless supper	Wheatless supper		Wheatless supper	Wheatless supper	Wheatless supper

W. A. Wiles, state hotel inspector and chairman of the hotel and restaurant committee of the Food Administration, noted that these were orders and not just requests.[72]

By December, the shortage of meat was becoming a serious concern for housewives. In a December 9, 1917, newspaper article titled "War Menus, Meatless Meals, Wheat Flour Substitutes," Ruth McLeod, government food conservation specialist, provided the following menu for a week's worth of meals, based on availability of products. McLeod noted that the use of coarser breads was good for the digestive system. In addition, she reminded the reader that dairy and poultry products, particularly cottage cheese and eggs, were necessary for the meatless diet.[73]

Breakfast	Dinner [a.k.a. Lunch]	Supper [a.k.a. Dinner]
Hominy, dates, milk, egg on toast, rye bread	Greens, stuffed baked potatoes, egg salad, corn bread, butter, preserves	Cream of tomato soup (made with skimmed milk), toasted bread sticks (made of left over bread), prune and walnut salad
Oatmeal with raisins and milk, poached egg on Graham toast	Brown rice, tomatoes, peppers en casserole, corn bread, cup custard (made with skimmed milk) with raisins	Cottage cheese, rye bread, apple sauce, oatmeal cookies
Grapes, poached eggs on toast	Twice cooked potatoes with cheese, buttered beets, fruit salad, potato bread	Brown rice and milk, soft boiled eggs, stewed prunes
Milk toast, stewed dried apples	Spinach soup (made with skimmed milk), baked soy beans, creamed onions, peppers stuffed with bread crumbs, corn bread	Chicken salad, lettuce, Graham crackers, cocoa
Apples, brown rice, raisins and milk, scrambled eggs, corn meal and muffins	Creamed eggs on Graham toast, sweet potato puff, okra and tomatoes, apple and nut salad	Peanut butter sandwiches (made with corn meal light bread), peaches and milk
Orange, boiled egg on Graham toast	Apples and sweet potatoes en casserole, spinach, egg salad, Graham gems, jelly	Cream of tomato soup (made with skimmed milk), fruit salad, brown bread
Oatmeal, prunes, Graham bread, glass of milk	Soy bean loaf with tomato sauce, salad	Vegetable soup, bread sticks, dried apricot salad
Milk toast, stewed dried apples	Salmon loaf (made using bread crumbs), pepper salad, cornmeal light bread	Mush and milk, pear salad, bran wafers
Cooked cracked wheat, raisins and milk, poached egg on Graham toast	Cabbage with cheese, baked potatoes, celery and apple salad, sweet potato bread	Celery soup (with croutons made of stale bread), baked apples, raisin cookies [74]

As 1917 ended and the new year began, the shortage of food would not be alleviated. In fact, the impending sugar shortage may have been the most difficult for Arkansans to accept.

Chapter 4: The Increasing Difficulty of Making Do in the Kitchen (1918)

"The victory will come to those who can hold out the longest, and food is the deciding factor in this case."[75]

In the published menu of Ruth McLeod, government food conservation specialist, eggs were the protein substitute of choice. However, by late 1917 and early 1918, home economists were encouraging Arkansas's housewives to increase preparation of cottage cheese and poultry as substitutes for red meat. *Cottage cheese* was even the word of the year in county agents' reports. Agents touted the nutritional benefits of the less expensive cottage cheese, one pound of which contained the protein equivalent of 1.27 pounds of sirloin steak or 1.58 pounds of loin pork chop. In 1918, the Cooperative Extension Service added a full-time cottage cheese specialist to its statewide staff.[76] In a May 1918 training school for twenty-five of the state's ninety county home demonstration agents from throughout Arkansas, one day's instruction dealt with the making, drying, and preparation of cottage cheese. The afternoon session included a menu of cottage cheese soup, sausage, roast, salad, and pie. According to the report, "a mere man would never have known what he was eating had his wife placed a dish of cottage cheese before him without explanation."[77] The federal government's pamphlet number 109, *Cottage Cheese Dishes*, gave recipes for the entrees, sides, and desserts practiced by the home demonstration agents.[78]

In March 1918, McLeod mentioned federal legislation requiring that wheat substitutes be purchased with every order of flour. The intent was that housewives would thus combine the substitutes with white flour in bread making. To her dismay, however, McLeod had learned that some housewives did not understand—or did not accept—the purpose and importance of the legislation. Instead, they went ahead and used the white flour for biscuits and filled their cupboards with the unopened oatmeal and cornmeal packages. McLeod shared a story about one woman who told her grocer that she would purchase the cornmeal because it was required, but she would feed it to her chickens. McLeod thus chastised housewives who failed to realize that using wheat substitutes was an important form of patriotism that the women could practice in their own homes. She continued, "The victory will come to those who can hold out the longest, and food is the deciding factor in this case."[79]

By the second half of 1918, sugar had become an endangered commodity. McLeod, whose title was now director of home economics for Arkansas of the U.S. Food Administration, offered a potpourri of advice even as the federal government made cuts to manufacturers. In late June, two Little Rock companies, the Kress Store at 612 Main and the Majestic Candy Kitchen at 800 Main, were required to give up 44,000 pounds of sugar to Williams, the state food administrator, because they failed to file a government report. The two merchants were denied sugar for the remainder of the year. In the same day's newspaper, an announcement was made of tighter restrictions on manufacturers of sugary products, from beverage syrups to sweet pickles, with a reduction in the sugar allowance from 80 percent to 50 percent of need. By now, households were allowed to buy no more than two pounds of sugar at one time.[80]

A couple of weeks later, the National Food Administration announced that there would be no interference with the fruit preserving season in the southern states because of the shortage. Refiners in the South were ordered by the National Food Administration not to ship any more sugar north of a line from Kansas City, Missouri, east to the northern boundary of North Carolina. Instead, the first to receive sugar would be the jobbers and retailers involved in the canning and preserving industry. Locally, McLeod noted that some cities in Arkansas were completely out of sugar. Because of the shortage, women had to preserve fruits with sugar substitutes, such as corn syrup, or by using only the sugar found in the fruit. As the months went by, McLeod offered other suggestions: boil the fruit pulp at least three times in jelly making; use the prune—a "patriotic food"—as a sugar saver and then save the pit for making gas masks; and eat locally, particularly the Arkansas sweet potato, which is more digestible when baked rather than boiled.[81]

On Sunday, September 22, McLeod shared candy recipes from the U.S. Food Administration in Washington DC. But first, she encouraged readers to be patriotic in their candy choices when purchasing candy from a downtown store. She noted that chocolate-covered cherries and nuts, peanut brittle made with molasses, and molasses caramels were likely to contain less sugar than chocolate creams, other cream candies, and mints. McLeod asked women to encourage their candy store managers to sell only war candies. She wished that every candy store would have a special case for war candies—which she referred to as sugarless treats—and would display them in the window rather than "cakes frosted exclusively with sugar and candies made exclusively from sugar."[82] McLeod then shared seven recipes, which are included in "Recipes for Making Do" on page 48.

Some of the substitutes through which families suffered indicate that the scarcity of sugar may have been the most difficult shortage for Arkansans to endure. In a disconcerting article in the October 6, 1918, *Arkansas Gazette*, McLeod encouraged housewives to use the more patriotic and less expensive corn sugar (not corn syrup) instead of granulated sugar. McLeod noted that in talking with housewives, however, she had become aware of little success with corn sugar. In her own experience, she had learned to use a very small amount of the sugar in the initial attempt at a recipe. Later, she would increase usage to the maximum amount that would give a palatable product. McLeod found that cooking fruits with corn sugar was usually not a good idea since the sugar's bitter flavor destroyed the natural fruit taste. However, it worked well sprinkled on grapefruit and other raw fruits. It was also palatable on oatmeal and mush, and she argued that one could learn to like it. She found that it lent itself best to the sweetening of milk products, such as custards and puddings. McLeod's corn sugar recipes[83] may be found in the "Recipes for Making Do" on page 49.

A large advertisement for Eatmore Cranberries on "The Woman's Page"[84] of the Sunday, October 13, 1918, *Arkansas Gazette* touted the many ways of preparing cranberries without using "so much sugar."[85] The advertisement noted that although cranberries were tasty and healthful, they had other selling points as well: no waste, no cores, no seeding, no peeling, and always acceptable. Most of the recipes used a combination of sugar and corn syrup, but the cranberry pie had a different twist:

Old Fashioned Cranberry Pie
Line a pie plate with short pastry. Sprinkle over this a little sugar, then fill with raw cranberries. Pour over them molasses, in proportion of ¼ cup molasses to each cup cranberries, and sift over top 2 level tablespoons flour. Wet edges of pie crust; cover cranberries with an upper crust and press edges closely together. Cut three slits in top and bake in moderate oven about 30 minutes.[86]

The cranberry pie recipe—with raw cranberries and molasses—along with McLeod's phrases, "it was also palatable"[87] and "one could learn to like it,"[88] indicate a somewhat desperate attempt among consumers to satisfy their collective sweet tooth.

Throughout Arkansas, county woman's committees reported on their food conservation activities. Although most did not provide specifics, the Bradley County committee noted that the chairman of home economics and food conservation and the county canning agent conducted wartime cooking demonstrations throughout the county. For several weeks, they taught classes at the high school. Using war food recipes carried in the newspaper, the county's various clubs discussed food conservation and substitutes for scarce commodities. Clubs and churches' missionary societies did away with having refreshments at their meetings. Several women planted gardens. In Crawford County, the home demonstration agent led the women of every community to organize in order to carry on food conservation work. The Home Economics Club of Van Buren met twice monthly to talk over conservation plans. Members then placed food made from substitutes in the window of a local store, after which they handed out recipes for the exhibited foods. During 1918, they gave demonstrations in twenty-nine communities and distributed 6,000 U.S. food leaflets. Stone County "stood 'behind the guns' when it came to food conservation and food production. Everyone planted larger gardens, and raised more chickens and hogs."[89]

In Union County, Irene Harper, of Junction City; Miss Huttig and Mrs. John Lewis, of Mount Holly; and Kate M. Hilliard, of El Dorado, all of whom were home economics graduates, "left no stone unturned in carrying out the advice of the government along food lines"[90] as they provided demonstrations of war bread and cakes around the county. The Randolph County report was particularly inspiring. The home demonstration agent visited towns and made stirring addresses before large audiences. Even during extremely bad weather, when the roads were almost impassable, she made long, up-country trips on horseback. The Randolph County report continued, "One day the horse fell through a defective culvert and threw [its] rider to the ground. Although both rider and horse sustained injuries, the determined woman mounted the faithful animal and rode on, fulfilling her appointments for the day and giving instructive talks on school gardening and demonstrations on making peanut butter and its use as a meat substitute."[91]

Although the counties' reports indicated only positive compliance with the government's conservation efforts, some newspaper articles reported Arkansans' resistance toward conservation, characterized as a lack of willingness to make sacrifices. For this reason, Mrs. C. E. Whitney's article on the AFWC page for October 28, 1917, in which she shared her own understanding of the need for the food conservation drive, is worth revisiting:

Our country has been wasteful and extravagant in the extreme. Luxuries had become necessities. There was an overabundance of

> many things and seemed to be no real necessity for rigid economy. Of course we had the poor ever with us, but the majority of American people were in more than comfortable circumstances. Both men and women drifted into extravagant and wasteful habits.[92]

Whitney's pep talk to Arkansas's women was right on target with historians' findings. During the prosperous period from 1876 to 1915, Americans' consumer habits gained significant momentum, as middle-class and working-class families had, according to historian Thomas Schlereth, "more money and more time to purchase more goods, mass-produced more cheaply and advertised more widely."[93] In addition, annual earnings rose during the period as weekly working hours declined—for example, factory workers saw their work week go from sixty-six hours in 1850 to fifty-five in 1914.[94] As the nation gradually shifted from a society of producers to one of consumers, the "'good' life came to mean the 'goods' life."[95] In his 1907 book *New Basis of Civilization*, theorist Simon N. Patten argued that until the mid-nineteenth century, every society had to cope with "an economy of scarcity."[96] But industrialization had made a surplus possible, and society's task was—for the first time in history—to live with much more.[97]

Although there were no newspaper reports revealing women's responses to the Little Rock master bakers' request to order bread in advance, some other practices point to a society that was self-indulgent and accustomed to having its way; as a result, its members had a difficult time adjusting to frugality. The tote-your-own-bundle campaign was likely met with disdain, as exemplified by Stifft's Jewelers' repeated requests, followed by its offers the following Christmas to donate a small sum to the Red Cross for each package carried home by the purchaser. Since, by 1915, American women accounted for almost 90 percent of all consumer spending,[98] the campaign was likely aimed at them. And some women displayed arrogance when, for example, they refused to combine prescribed substitutes with wheat in their bread making. When restaurant, hotel, and boarding house owners initially allowed consumers the choice of compliance or noncompliance, consumers chose the latter. Later, candy store owners, who were not required to follow the government's conservation guidelines, bowed to patrons' wishes for sugary desserts.

Recipes for Making Do

The following recipes were taken from the U.S. Department of Agriculture Circular 109, *Cottage Cheese Dishes*, 1918:

How to Make Cottage Cheese
1 gallon of skimmed milk
1 cupful of buttermilk or thick, sour milk for a starter
⅛ of a junket tablet dissolved in 2 tablespoonsful of water
(For fuller directions see Farmers' Bulletin 850, "How to Make Cottage Cheese on the Farm," which may be obtained free on application to the Secretary of Agriculture, Washington DC)

Sauces for Creamed and Scalloped Dishes
Cottage-cheese sauces are useful for creaming potatoes, eggs, toast and leftover vegetables, and for scalloping those and other dishes. The cheese thickens the sauce somewhat. Unless the acid is neutralized with baking soda, it tends to curdle the sauce and gives it a slight sour or acid flavor. From ¼ to ¾ teaspoon of soda is necessary to neutralize completely the acid flavor in one cup of cheese. The soda should be dissolved in a little milk or hot water, and blended with the cheese. Use the soda carefully, as too much is as bad as too little.

Proportions for White Sauces with Cottage Cheese

Consistency	Milk	Butter	Flour	Salt	Pepper	Cheese
Thin Sauce	1 cup	1/2 tbsp.	1/2 tbsp.	1/3 tsp.	dash	1/4 cup
Med. Sauce	1 cup	1/2 tbsp.	1 tbsp.	1/3 tsp.	dash	1/4 cup
Thick Sauce	1 cup	1 tbsp.	2 tbsp.	1/2 tsp.	dash	1/4 cup

Cottage Cheese and Peanut-Butter Soup

Make thin cottage-cheese sauce (use preceding directions), neutralizing the acid of the cottage cheese with baking soda. Blend the peanut butter with the cheese before adding the sauce, using 1 tablespoon peanut butter for each cup of the sauce. Season with a slice of onion, a bit of bay leaf, and a pinch of powdered sage heated with the milk.

Creamy Eggs with Cottage Cheese

1 cup milk   1 T. butter

1 T. flour   ⅛ t. pepper

4 eggs   1 t. salt

1 cup cottage cheese   Paprika

¼ t. soda   Parsley, or pimientos

Make a thick sauce with the milk, flour, butter, and seasonings. Cook 5 minutes and pour gradually on the cheese, which has been neutralized with the soda dissolved in a little of the milk. When the cheese and sauce are well blended, return them to the top of the double boiler and reheat over hot water. Beat the eggs slightly, pour them into the warm sauce, and mix well. As the mixture sets in a soft custard on the bottom and sides of the boiler, scrape it up carefully, forming large, soft curds. The mixture is cooked when it is of a creamy consistency throughout. This quantity will serve eight or more persons.

Cottage-Cheese Loaf with Nuts

2 cups cottage cheese   1 T. fat
1 cup chopped nuts (see variations)   Salt, pepper
1 cup cold leftover cereal (any kind)
⅓ t. soda or more to neutralize acid
1 cup dry bread crumbs
Sage, poultry seasoning, or mixed herbs
2 T. chopped onion, or ½ t. onion juice
Worcestershire sauce, or kitchen bouquet if desired

Mix all ingredients together thoroughly and bake in a buttered pan in a hot oven till top and sides are well browned over. Turn out on a hot platter. Serve with a brown or tomato sauce if desired.

Variations: This loaf is particularly good made with peanuts. Substitute for the cup of chopped nuts in the rule above, 4 T. of peanut butter and ½ cup of coarsely chopped nuts, and season with ½ t. of ground sage or with 1 t. of mixed poultry seasoning. If walnuts are used, pimientos make a good garnish.

Cottage-Cheese Loaf with Beans or Peas

1 cup cottage cheese
2 T. chopped onion or ½ t. onion juice
¼ t. soda to neutralize acid
2 cups cooked beans
2 T. savory fat
1 cup boiled rice (dry)
Chopped celery or celery salt, or pimientos, or Worcestershire sauce, or mixed poultry seasoning
1 cup dry bread crumbs

Peas and small lima beans may be used whole. Mash larger beans or put them through the meat chopper. Mix beans, cheese, bread crumbs, and seasoning together well and form into a roll. The roll should be mixed very stiff, as the cheese softens when heated. Bake in a moderate oven, basting occasionally with a well-flavored fat. Serve with tomato or other sauce.

Cottage Cheese Sandwich Fillings

Cottage cheese may be used as a sandwich filling, taking the place of meat or egg filling. Rye, graham, and Boston brown bread lend themselves well to cottage-cheese sandwiches.

Variations: The cheese may be combined with nuts, grated cheese, pimientos, horse-radish, chopped or sliced olives, whole or chopped nuts, sliced celery, chives, Spanish onions, raisins, dates, prunes softened by soaking, freshly crushed mint leaves, honey, jelly, or marmalade. These additions may be blended with the cheese or may be spread in a layer over it.

Cottage-Cheese Tarts or Pie

1 ½ cups cottage cheese	⅓ cup sugar
Whites of 2 eggs beaten stiff	Lemon juice
½ cup heavy cream, whipped	Few gratings of lemon rind

To the cottage cheese add part of the whipped cream, and the flavoring, which should be very delicate. Fold in last the beaten egg whites. Heap lightly into ready-cooked, delicately browned pastry cases, made by baking pie crust in muffin tins or on the bottom of an inverted pie tin. Garnish the top of the tarts or pie with the rest of the whipped cream, and with fresh or canned fruit if desired. This makes a large one-crust pie or 12 tarts.

Variation: Cinnamon or nutmeg may be substituted for lemon in the recipe given above.

Fresh, dried, or canned fruits may be folded into the filling just before serving, or the top may be garnished with jelly or marmalade or with fresh fruit lightly dusted with powdered sugar. The filling may be used by itself as a dessert, piled lightly in glass cups or tall glasses, and garnished with preserved or fresh fruit.

Cottage-Cheese Pie

1 cup cottage cheese	1 T. melted fat
⅔ cup sugar	Salt
⅔ cup milk (see note below)	¼ t. vanilla
2 egg yolks, beaten	

Mix the ingredients in the order given. Bake the pie in one crust. Cool it slightly and cover it with meringue made by adding 2 T. of sugar and ½ t. of vanilla to the beaten whites of 2 eggs and brown it in a slow oven.—New York State College of Agriculture

Note: One T. of cornstarch stirred smoothly into the milk will prevent the custard from separating in the oven.

Old Dutch-Cheese Cake

1 cup cottage cheese	2 T. cornstarch
⅔ cup sugar	1 T. melted fat
½ cup milk	Salt
2 eggs	¼ t. lemon juice

Mix the ingredients in the order given. Mace or nutmeg may be used for flavoring. Bake 25 minutes in a moderate oven until brown. This makes a very firm custard.

The last page of the booklet featured uses of whey, with menus for whey syrup, whey lemonade and punch, whey-cornstarch pudding, and Bavarian cream.[99]

The following recipes were found in an article titled "Prepare Breakfast Food at Home, Save More Wheat," *Arkansas Gazette*, December 30, 1917:

Cornmeal Mush

1 ½ cups cornmeal (not bolted)	5 to 6 cups water
2 level teaspoons salt	

Add the meal gradually to the boiling salted water. Let boil at least 15 minutes, stirring constantly, then place in double boiler and cook several hours, or place in the fireless cooker. [100]

Note: If one does not possess a double boiler, improvise one by placing a small vessel into a larger one filled with boiling water. A vessel inserted in the top of the teakettle often serves such a purpose.

Oatmeal
1 cup oatmeal
3 cups water
½ teaspoon salt
½ cup raisins or prunes

Add the oatmeal to the rapidly boiling salted water. Boil five minutes, then place in a double boiler and cook for one hour or place in the fireless cooker overnight. Add the raisins, dates, or prunes to the cereal 10 minutes before removing it from the fire. Fruits added to the breakfast food help to prevent constipation. A few tablespoons of bran sprinkled over the breakfast food will serve the same purpose.

Brown Rice
One cup brown rice, 3 cups water, 1 teaspoon salt

The brown rice should be looked over, washed in a sieve and then added gradually to rapidly boiling water. Let boil for one hour, then let dry out and serve. Try and have as little water as is possible at the end of the cooking. Drain the rice and let dry out so as to separate the grains. Never throw away any liquid from the brown rice and use it in soup making, bread making, etc.

Bran or Liberty Muffins
One cup bran, one cup cornmeal, one cup white flour, one egg, one tablespoon syrup, one tablespoon shortening, one teaspoon salt, three teaspoons baking powder, water or milk to make batter.

Mix the dry ingredients, then add the beaten egg, syrup and shortening, then milk to make a batter.

Note: If sour milk is used, add ⅛ to ¼ teaspoon soda to each cup sour milk, varying the amount of soda according to how sour the milk is.

Bran Bread
(Government Bulletin)

Five teaspoons molasses, one-half teaspoon salt, one cup sweet milk, one-fourth teaspoon soda, one cup white flour, two cups bran and four teaspoons baking powder.

Sift and measure flour. Add salt, soda and milk to molasses; sift baking powder into flour and add bran; mix with liquid, beating thoroughly, and turn into well-greased pans. Bake in moderate oven 30 or 40 minutes.

50 Per Cent Cornmeal Biscuits
(Hannah Wessling)

Two cups cornmeal, two cups white flour, four teaspoons baking powder, two teaspoons salt, four teaspoons shortening, liquid to mix to proper consistency (1 to 1 ½ cups)

Sift together the flour, salt and baking powder, add cornmeal. Have the shortening as cold as possible and cut it into the mixture with a knife, finally rubbing it in with the hands. Mix quickly with cold liquid (milk, skim milk, or water), forming a fairly soft dough, which can be rolled on the board. Turn on to a floured board; roll into sheet and over one half inch thick; cut into rounds, place these in lightly floured biscuit tins (or shallow pans) and bake 10 to 12 minutes in rather hot oven.

50 Per Cent Oatmeal Biscuits

Use same recipe as above, but substitute oatmeal in the place of cornmeal.

Potato Cornmeal Muffins

Two tablespoons fat, one tablespoon sugar, one egg, well beaten; one cup milk, one cup mashed potatoes, one cup cornmeal, four teaspoons baking powder and one teaspoon salt.

Mix in order given, bake 40 minutes in hot oven. This makes 12 muffins. They are delicious.

The following recipes were found in an article titled "To Make Candy Without Sugar," *Arkansas Gazette*, Sunday, September 22, 1918:

Stuffed Dates

Use the best dates. Remove the stones. Fill with peanuts, walnuts, hickory nuts or any nut available. Peanut butter makes a good filling that is different. Press dates in shape and roll in chopped nuts, coconut, or a mixture of coconut and powdered cinnamon.

Stuffed Prunes

Steam one pound prunes and remove stones. Stuff part of the prunes, each with another prune, stuff other with chopped salted nuts or stuff with a mixture of one cup each raisins and walnuts and a few candied cherries. Another suggestion is to stuff prunes with stiff orange marmalade.

Candied Drirambo[101]

One cup cooking apples, fourth cup syrup, fourth cup water, nuts.

Cook apples as for sauce. Add fourth cup corn syrup and cook until a thick paste. Nuts may be added. Spread out in buttered pan. Dry out in oven or over oven for half day. Use other fruits in the same way.

Candied Apples

One pound [apples] (which do not cook readily). Peel and cut into size desired. Drop into one cup of syrup and boil slowly until apple becomes transparent. Take apple out a piece at a time and drain on fork. Let stand on wax paper three-fourth hours, roll in coconut. Other fruits may be used in place of apples.

The following recipes were found in an article titled "How Corn Sugar May be Utilized," *Arkansas Gazette*, Sunday, October 6, 1918:

Corn Sugar Rice Pudding
Two cups cooked rice
Half cup raisins
Two cups custard made with corn sugar

Prepare two cups of corn sugar custard according to above recipe. Pour this over two cups of rice and a half cup of raisins; bake 30 minutes in a very slow oven.

Corn Sugar Bread Pudding
One and one-half cups of toasted bread crumbs
Two cups custard made with corn sugar
Half cup raisins
Pinch of salt

Dry out the bread in an oven until a very light brown, then roll with a rolling pin. Add this, together with half cup of raisins, to two cups of the corn sugar custard. Bake in a slow oven for 30 minutes.

Note—A sauce made of corn syrup and corn starch may be served with this pudding if desired.

Corn Sugar Chocolate Pudding.
Two cups custard made with corn sugar
Half cake of melted bitter chocolate
Two tablespoons of cornstarch
Vanilla flavoring
Melt the bitter chocolate and add to the corn sugar custard. Next

mix the cornstarch with one-quarter cup of cold water and stir into the custard. Cook in a double boiler (or over hot water), stirring constantly to prevent lumping. Cook until thick enough to coat a spoon. Let cool and serve.

Chapter 5: Doing Their Bit for the Boys

"My son is at Vancouver barracks in the regular army. I'm expecting a telegram from him daily saying he has started for Cuba or France. When he gets on the ocean I think I'll have to come down here and work all day long to keep from worrying about him."[102]

When the United States entered the war, it was not prepared to provide warm winter clothing for its soldiers, who would soon be in the trenches in France, or to deliver surgical and medical supplies for its hospitalized wounded. Although Red Cross chapters had been conducting war work of various sorts since 1914, with the United States' entry into the war, the demand for supplies "leaped hundredfold."[103] There were no choices other than for U.S. women to construct millions of needed pieces of sewn and knitted items. The Red Cross Woman's Bureau (usually called simply the Woman's Bureau) was created in July 1917 primarily to direct the energies of the millions of eager-to-serve wives, sisters, and mothers of members of the U.S. Army and Navy forces. Women's desire to be of service would lead to "wasteful chaos"[104] if their work was not organized, standardized, and focused on meeting the specific needs of French relief organizations and hospitals.[105]

The Arkansas chapter of the American Red Cross and the Arkansas Woman's Committee complemented one another's responsibilities. Often the same women were working for both entities. Women's organizations retained social connections with their members, who cooperated under the auspices of the Red Cross to knit or sew for troops. Women of church organizations throughout the state,[106] various chapters of the Daughters of the American Revolution, and members of the National Society of Colonial Dames of America—to name only a few representative groups—reported that their members spent untold hours in the workrooms to provide hospital supplies, knitted socks, sweaters, and wristlets for "the boys."[107] The women's suffrage organizations in Arkansas noted that "the majority of the organizations in the State almost discontinued their suffrage activities in order that their members might give their time to work in Red Cross rooms, to the sale of Liberty Bonds and War Savings Stamps."[108]

By June 1917—even before the Red Cross Woman's Bureau was established—Arkansas's women were already making thousands of pieces of hospital supplies as U.S. troops prepared to sail for France. In Little Rock, the Gus Blass and M. M. Cohn companies' display windows exhibited complete outfits needed for hospitalized soldiers. A newspaper article explained:

> One complete outfit consists of six sheets, four draw shirts, two spreads, four pillow cases, four pajama suits, three hospital bed shirts, one convalescent gown, four pairs of socks, two pairs bed socks, four bath towels, three face towels, one wash cloth, one pair slippers, one hot water bag cover, one ice water bag cover and six handkerchiefs.[109]

Thus, each hospitalized soldier required forty-six pieces of sewn or knitted supplies, thousands of which were made in Red Cross workrooms throughout Arkansas.

Workrooms provided two major types of work for women: one, items needed for military hospitals' patients and personnel—including the highly precise construction of surgical bandages; two, knitted articles to protect soldiers from the cold. After making suggestions as to the kind of warm materials needed for convalescent robes, the Woman's Bureau established standards for hospital garments, pajamas, bathrobes, surgeons' and nurses' operating gowns and masks, hospital bed shirts, undershirts, bed socks, underdrawers, and hot water and ice bag covers. The next step was to make arrangements for eight large pattern companies to cut patterns for the authorized garments. Patterns would be for sale through normal retail channels and in Red Cross chapter rooms.[110]

Enlisting instructors for the difficult surgical dressings work was an immediate concern for the American Red Cross. Under a New York physician's supervision, twenty-three standard dressings were selected, and the bureau issued two circulars nationwide. One described each dressing in detail, with diagram; the second was for instructors. Because of rapidly increasing numbers of Red Cross chapters and members, the complicated task of training a sufficient cadre of local trainers in bandage-making was another vital concern for the bureau. By selecting and training laywomen to train the local trainers, the Woman's Bureau hoped to limit any additional burden placed on nurses, whose numbers had decreased as many readied to sail for France. Another priority for the bureau was to select other able, hard-working women to supervise the day-to-day workroom production activities. These supervisors would face challenges, as, according to author Ida Clyde Clarke, "the work is being constantly interrupted by new workers who do not know what it is all about— women who want to knit and have to be taught to knit, women who want to sew and have to be taught to sew."[111]

While Arkansas's women were diligently making items for military hospitals in France, the head of the Red Cross Commission in France cabled the Woman's Bureau to report an "imperative need,"[112] before Christmas, for knitted sweaters, socks, mufflers, and wristlets for all men in the trenches during the harsh French winter, with its expected fuel shortages. After consulting with authorities from the British, Canadian, and French Red Cross organizations, as well as knitting experts from women's magazines and commercial mills, the Woman's Bureau issued half a million circulars with simple directions for knitting four items most needed in France: a bed sock, an aviator's helmet, a hot water bottle cover, and a wash rag.[113] The best wool for the purpose and price would be four-ply No. 10, in gray and khaki. Although the Red Cross provided standardized patterns and recommended the choice of wool, the organization accepted articles that were not up to its standards; however, the thinking was that the only way the average woman could be sure of coming as near as possible to providing the needed product was to follow the detailed instructions.[114]

By late August, the Woman's Bureau sent a rush order to Arkansas's workrooms for knitted articles for soldiers on the front lines in France. The urgent request noted that U.S. and allied soldiers would suffer from the bitter cold during the winter, partly because of a lack of warm housing accommodations. Soldiers would need warm clothing next to their bodies—particularly woolen socks, sweaters, and wristlets. The letter requested that workrooms engaged in making surgical supplies switch immediately to knitting clothing articles instead. Women who were not part of an organized workroom were asked to knit according to the Red Cross instructions published in the news article.[115]

In late October, the Little Rock workroom's surgical supplies supervisor reported that she had recently shipped 21,498 dressings to the Bureau of Supplies in St. Louis, a sufficient number for a 500-bed base hospital. The workroom was completing an average of 1,500 dressings each week. During the same October week, workers completed 69 bed shirts, 44 pajama suits, 18 pajama pants, 30 convalescent robes, 32 towels, 39 pillow cases, 33 operating sheets, 29 pairs of socks, 72 sweaters, 57 mufflers, and 78 pairs of wristlets. Members of the Pulaski County Community Club, to whom wool was distributed on October 1, had already completed 46 knitted articles.[116]

In early December, however, the St. Louis district of the Red Cross, which encompassed Arkansas, received orders to provide 600,000 surgical dressings—which were different from those already being made—to be received in New York by January 1 for shipment to France. In order to meet the deadline, Arkansas's workrooms' hours were increased to include evening work as well as the daytime schedule.[117] Bradley County's final report is a good example to represent the women in Arkansas's seventy-five counties, who worked hours upon hours in Red Cross workrooms during the war: "Number of work rooms in county, 2; number of knitting units in county, 20; work room chairmen included cutting, knitting, and surgical dressing. Work room report: knitted goods, 1,002; hospital garments, 1,124; surgical dressings, 5,755; refugee garments, 239; total,

9,020."[118] One mother was representative of numerous women who labored daily in Red Cross workrooms: "My son is at Vancouver barracks in the regular army. I'm expecting a telegram from him daily saying he has started for Cuba or France. When he gets on the ocean I think I'll have to come down here and work all day long to keep from worrying about him."[119]

Nationally, Clarke reported, "Refreshment corps have established canteens along the railroad lines, so that soldiers en route to camps, cantonments, and transports, should have sandwiches and hot drinks, and a chance to mail letters as they passed through."[120] In their final reports, several Arkansas counties' woman's committees made brief comments regarding local Red Cross canteen work. Conway County reported that, as Company D of the Arkansas National Guard was trained in Morrilton, "many entertainments were given for their benefit."[121] The woman's committee also provided canteen service for troops en route. Jefferson County noted that "the canteen service has proven a great help and inspiration to the troops of soldiers passing through Pine Bluff."[122] In Polk County, a canteen committee of five women sent out library books each month to the army camps, and members passed out periodicals to soldiers passing through Mena. The health and recreation department of the Washington County Woman's Committee cooperated with the canteen committee of the Red Cross in providing "a musical, an automobile ride, and box lunches for the departing selectives."[123] Although Crawford County did not mention its Red Cross canteen work, the photograph of women and young men waiting at the train station in Van Buren (page 90) is more than sufficient.[124]

Despite the Red Cross Woman's Bureau's massive organizational and communications structure, its workrooms were not tasked with providing for every need of the U.S. Army and Navy or for the staggering requirements among the nation's allies. In order to provide for certain unmet needs, individual women's organizations stepped up to fill the void. For its contribution, the Arkansas Society of the Daughters of the American Revolution, with 600 members throughout the state, chose to provide a sweater for Christmas for members of the Arkansas National Guard who were in training camps, many at Camp Beauregard in Alexandria, Louisiana. Both Governor Brough and General Lloyd England, Arkansas's Adjutant General, endorsed the movement, since the government did not furnish sweaters to Arkansas's 6,169 National Guard members. The organization asked women who could not knit to donate yarn or money. Women willing to knit but unable to afford the yarn would receive yarn at no cost. If a sweater was designated for a certain soldier, every effort would be made to see that it reached him.[125]

Although the sweater campaign was announced on November 4—less than two months before Christmas—women throughout the state responded to the call. The Arkansas Synodical Auxiliary of the Presbyterian Church, which was gathered at the time of the announcement, as well as women in several Arkansas towns, organized within the first week. The sweaters would be sent to the Arkansas Guard members by December 20, which would ensure their arrival before Christmas Day. The organization called on mothers, sisters, and sweethearts of Guard members to help in the enormous undertaking. The committee asked women to enclose a self-addressed postcard with each sweater so that the recipient might acknowledge the gift. In its final report, the DAR reported that 500 sweaters were presented to the trainees.[126]

Despite the Red Cross's responsibility to provide warm clothing for soldiers fighting in France, no one was assigned the task of knitting for members of the U.S. Navy serving on oceangoing vessels. The Navy League of the United States saw a need that its members could meet and immediately sent out representatives to establish branches in every state. The Arkansas branch's specific goal was to enlist recruits to knit woolen garments for the 1,600 men, including officers, of the USS *Arkansas*. On July 1, 1917, the *Arkansas Gazette* printed directions, sent out by the American Red Cross and Comforts Committee of the Navy League, for women who could knit at home but could not get away to knit at specific times in organized gatherings.[127]

The organization was able to provide each crew member with a knitted sweater, helmet, and wristlet before December 1, 1917. Most of the organization's work ended as the Red Cross took charge of the bulk of knitting operations with the beginning of 1918. All in all, the Arkansas chapter of the Navy League knitted about 6,000 garments. During the same period, however, another state women's organization was working diligently to provide for an additional unmet need for the men of the USS *Arkansas*.[128]

During the first year after the completion of the battleship USS *Arkansas*, which was commissioned in 1912, the Woman's Christian Temperance Union of Arkansas (WCTU) was asked to furnish comfort bags for its sailors. Members of the organization provided 1,000 bags, a sufficient number at that time. By 1917, however, there were 1,600 naval personnel on the ship, and the WCTU set about to furnish bags for all personnel by September 15. The organization welcomed others who wished to make the bags, but it advised that all bags must come through the organization. For those women who did not have access to a local union with which to work, directions were printed in state newspapers. Monetary contributions were greatly appreciated, and Sunday School teachers were urged to include the young members of their classes in the project.[129]

Although most of the women's volunteer work was accomplished for the benefit of the United States' men fighting in Europe, one organization's goal was to help the children of France in particular. In November 1917, a group of Arkansans formed a committee to join in one national effort to make at least a small dent in what many Americans considered a moral obligation owed to the French people, who had made great sacrifices in the war effort since 1914. At the initial meeting, participants committed to provide funds for forty-three French children through the "Fatherless Children of France" program, which was organized in 1915 and had grown to 200 committees throughout the United States by the end of the war. Although some men were included in the organizational meeting, the effort was recorded in the Report of the Arkansas Woman's Committee. In a newspaper article on November 24, 1917, one member of the committee explained it this way:

> The object is to conserve the homes of France. The French government allows a pension of twenty-three cents to the soldier's widow and ten cents a day for each child, which sum is insufficient. The French committee has found that by adding ten cents a day to the fund the careful French mother is enabled to give her children nourishing food and the barest necessities and keep them together in her home.[130]

Thus, the goal of the organization was to provide $36.50 yearly—ten cents per day—to allow each French child to remain at home and under his or her mother's care. Individuals and organizations were furnished the names of the children whom they "adopted." In Fordyce, in Dallas County, one club took the name Eugenie Avauzelle—in honor of the French girl whom members supported.[131] Mississippi County reported that school children of the county had adopted twenty children. The number included two African American schools, at Blytheville and Wilson.[132] In the final few months of the war, however, "the terrible summer of 1918 placed on the lists of the Paris committee 250,000 orphans, and a call was sent out asking that this number be apportioned to the various committees, to the end that this vast number should not plead in vain."[133] As a result, Arkansas was asked to provide for an additional 4,000 children at a total annual cost of $146,000.[134]

To meet the massive, immediate need, an administrative board—including Governor Brough and other prominent citizens of the state—provided financial backing. The Council of Defense for Arkansas sent out requests for support, and each county was given a quota. Phillips County was lauded in the report as the banner county; with a quota of 191, the county "adopted" 315 children. As the Arkansas Woman's Committee's report, through December 30, 1918, was completed and ready to mail, Mrs. E. G. Thompson, committee chairman, noted that 3,663 of the 4,000 children had been adopted. Thompson expressed hope that the remaining children would be provided for within a week's time.[135]

Instructions for Doing

Comfort Bags[136]

Take dark blue denim or strong, pretty cretonne, one yard in width, cut off one yard and three inches for six bags, 18 inches wide and 13 inches long before being made; double the goods and take double seam across bottom and up one side; work buttonhole on seam and on opposite side 4 inches from top, then turn down 2 inches for hem, which comes below buttonhole on wrong side; stitch edge of hem, also 1 inch above, then run in two pieces of tape, each 21 inches long, sew ends together, then draw up like handbag. Before stitching hem, make pocket for buttons, baste to position underneath edge of hem; baste needle flap, consisting of three pieces of new flannel, red, white and blue, on opposite side under hem. Sew pieces of tape underneath and on top of needle flap, so that it can be rolled up.

Contents of Bag

2 sizes of black and white buttons	1 flat disc pin cushion or pin ball, filled with pins
1 spool basting thread	
1 spool white thread No. 24	1 small roll gauze 2 inches in width
1 spool black thread No. 24	1 small package absorbent cotton
1 spool white darning cotton	1 small package adhesive plaster
1 spool black darning cotton	1 pledge card
1 pair small blunt scissors	8 [3?] good leaflets
6 needles No. 5	1 Testament
6 coarse darning needles	1 Red, White and Blue Songster
6 safety pins	A good, motherly letter, with self-addressed postcard
1 piece narrow tape	

For Knitting Mufflers[137]

Cast on 50 inches or 10 inches.

Plain knitting for 58 inches.

No. 5 celluloid needle. Dark blue knitting yarn—two hanks.

For Knitting Wristlets[138]

Cast on 52 stitches.

Knit two, purl two for 12 inches.

Sew up, leaving two-inch space for thumb two inches from top.

No. 3 bone needle. Gray knitting yarn—one-half hank.

Sleeveless Jacket No. 8044[139]

Two hanks (or four balls) Bear brand knitting worsted, gray or blue; one pair Bucilla amber needles, size 5; five stitches to an inch.

Cast on 80 inches loosely, knit two, purl two for four inches or about 30 rows and knit plain until work measures 23 inches. Next row knit 26 stitches, knit and bind off loosely next 28 stitches and on the remaining 26 stitches knit 10 ribs (20 rows) back and forth for left shoulder. The last row will bring yarn to neck side. Break off. Beginning at neck knit 10 ribs on stitches reserved for right shoulder, cast on 28 stitches opposite those bound of for neck and knit the 26 stitches on left shoulder, when all 80 stitches will again be on needle. Knit plain for 19 inches and finish with four inches of knit two, purl two to match beginning of jacket. Bind off loosely, sew up sides and leave nine inches open for armholes.

Sock No. 8047[140]

One and one-half hanks (or three balls) Bear brand knitting worsted, gray only; five steel needles size 11.

Leg—Cast 18 stitches on each of four needles, join, work in a ribbing of knit two, purl two for four inches and then knit plain until work measures 13 inches.

Heel—Take half the number of stitches (36), on one needle for the heel (leaving 18 stitches on each of the instep needles), and on the 36 stitches knit one row, purl one row alternately for 30 rows, always slipping the first stitch. Begin to turn heel on wrong side. Purl 20, purl two together, turn; slip first stitch, purl 5, purl two together, turn; slip 1, knit six, slip 1, knit 1, pass slipped stitch over knitted stitch, turn and continue working toward the sides of heel in this manner, having one more stitch between decreases on every row until all the stitches are worked in. There should then be 20 stitches on needle.

Gussets—Pick up and knit 15 stitches on left edge of heel, knit the two instep needles, pick up and knit 15 stitches on right edge of heel, on the same needle knit 10 of the heel stitches and slip the remaining 10 heel stitches on the next needle. There will now be 25 stitches on each of the heel needles and 16 stitches on each of the instep needles. Knit one even round and in next round decrease as follows: Knit together the second and third stitches from end of first needle, work across instep needles, on last needle knit one, slip one, knit one, pass the slipped stitch over the knitted stitch and knit to end. Decrease in this manner every second round until there are 16 stitches left on each heel needle.

Knit even until foot measures seven inches from heel.

Toe—Knit to the last three stitches on first needle, knit two together, knit one; on second needle, knit one, slip one, knit one, pass slipped stitch over knitted stitch, knit to end; on third needle knit to the last three stitches, knit two together, knit one, on last needle, knit one, slip one, knit one, pass the slipped stitch over the knitted stitch and knit to end. Knit three rounds even, one decreasing round, 2 rounds even, one decreasing round, 2 rounds even, 1 decreasing round, one round even and then decrease in every round until there are eight stitches left. Put the four stitches on sole side on one needle, the four stitches of upper side on another needle and sew together with joining stitch given below.

Joining Stitch—Thread a darning needle and bring pieces to be joined close together. Draw up yarn in first stitch on upper piece, inserting needle from wrong side; insert needle from right side in first stitch on lower piece and bring up through next stitch from wrong side—draw up yarn; * insert needle from right side in same stitch as before on lower piece and bring up through next stitch—draw up yarn; repeat from * until all stitches are joined and fasten yarn well before breaking off.

For Knitting Helmets[141]

One fourth pound knitting yarn—two celluloid needles No. 3 ½; four steel needles No. 11 or size smaller than celluloid needles.

With celluloid needles cast on 54 stitches, knit plain 10 inches for front; slip off on spare needle. Work another piece to correspond, five inches for back.

Slip the stitches of both pieces onto three steel needles, having 36 stitches on each needle; knit two, purl two for five inches; bind off 30 stitches very loosely to make the opening for the face; knit two, purl two, forward and backward for thirteen rows.

Cast on 30 stitches loosely, and on three needles knit two, purl two for two and one-half inches. Knit one round plain, then narrow by knitting the last two stitches on each needle, together, every row, until there are eight stitches left on each needle; then knit two stitches together all around, leaving four stitches on each needle; then draw loop of the yarn through all twelve stitches, with a crochet hook and fasten firmly. Knit rather snugly.

Finished articles to be sent to the Navy League of the United States, Southern building, Washington, D.C.

Chapter 6: Taking New Jobs or Keeping the Old

"The right to earn a living and the right to live are indistinguishable terms. We are told that wages of women need not be adequate for their support, as many of the girls and women live at home. When this fact is given by the employer, he admits he is not paying a living wage, as the brother or father has to supply what he refuses to pay."[142]

The United States' entry into the Great War opened up opportunities for women to enter into employment in positions in which they had not previously worked. In addition, women were asserting their rights for fair treatment and wages in positions traditionally reserved for them. And the Arkansas Woman's Committee found itself acting as an advocate for female workers as employers attempted to push the envelope in requiring them to work under unacceptable conditions. Throughout the war, even the "Help Wanted—Female" section of local newspapers gave small hints that women were needed in additional areas of work. From the March 5, 1917, *Arkansas Gazette*, at which time the United States was close to entering the war, came this disconcerting list of positions for women:

Chambermaid
Unencumbered woman to keep house and do general house work
White woman to do housework in private family; nice room
Neat appearing young lady for theatrical novelty
A white woman for general housework
Waitress and cooks — German girl $5 week; colored cook with reference $5; 19 domestics $3 to $5 week
White housekeeper
Six girls for road show; must have neat appearance; good salary and sure pay
Good, experienced pantry woman
Girl or woman for light housework
German cook, a woman without children $5 week, board and room[143]

Traditionally, the "Help Wanted—Female" column included positions in private homes and small businesses; the road show opportunities were an interesting twist. As the war ran its course, newspapers' help-wanted ads for women changed very little. However, similar columns, dated June 1, 1917, and December 24, 1917, no longer mentioned positions for German women. The June column included a position for a young lady, experienced in bookkeeping and stenography, and the December column advertised a vacant position for a lady, combination stenographer and clerk, willing to live at a sawmill in a good locality.[144]

Throughout 1917, newspaper articles addressed the need for women workers, and national columnists offered advice to women considering a field of employment previously occupied by men. Although most vacancies were in industrial states, articles titled "Girls Work In Bloomers; More Safe and Sanitary than Skirts,"[145] "Never So Much Work for Women as Now; Those Working for Wedding Rings Barred,"[146] and "War Work is Teaching Women the True Worth of Their World's Work"[147] provided rhetorical insights into major changes for women throughout the nation. As a rural state with a small population, Arkansas did not have the great need for women workers confronted by large, industrial states; however, during the war, almost 1,000 Arkansas women worked in saw and planing mills, box factories, and certain lines of railroad and office work.[148]

During the summer of 1917, women were already performing light duties in Arkansas's sawmills. Since they were not working more than nine hours in a day, there was no violation of state women's employment laws. However, in July, a Kensett, Arkansas, lumber company manager submitted a request to the state deputy labor commissioner, asking for approval to hire women to work for ten hours of light duty a day. The manager noted that the women were willing to work the extended hours. The deputy commissioner did not allow the women to work more than nine hours daily, citing a request from the National Woman's Committee, which asked the state agency to enforce laws for the protection of women in industry.

"The council takes the position that to grant longer hours would be drawing upon the vitality of future generations, and that at this time it is imperative to conserve not only the national resources, but the human as well."[149]

The National Woman's Committee's response was consistent with its emphasis on the health and well-being of future generations—as is exemplified in chapter eleven, "Making Things Better for the Children"—and emphasized women's role as guardians of the nation's future. According to the letter, the sawmill manager was not allowed to have the women work for ten hours daily solely because of possible detriment to their future children.[150] The concept was consistent with laws and practices of the era.[151] The underlying justification for protective legislation for women was that "the future of the country depended upon their ability to bear healthy children."[152]

As the state women in industry department of the Arkansas Woman's Committee became functional, it was tasked with overseeing female employees to ensure that they were placed "where they would render most efficient service."[153] Women were urged to remain in their own localities without changing from one position to another.[154] However, historians have reported that women were already a fixture within the workforce by the time of the war. In fact, the number of single women who worked before marriage rose from 20 percent in 1850 to 50 percent by 1900.[155]

The women in industry department was also charged with advocating for women and thus focused on ensuring appropriate working conditions. Governor Brough appointed Mary H. McCabe, state chairman of the department, as Secretary of Minimum Wage and Maximum Hour, an action that provided McCabe authority to meet the needs of Arkansas's women in the workplace. McCabe and her department worked to ensure that the Minimum Wage and Maximum Hour Law was enforced throughout the state. Partial inspections were made at Little Rock, Fort Smith, Fayetteville, Pine Bluff, Newport, Searcy, Harrison, Magnolia, Arkadelphia, Jonesboro,

Batesville, and Paragould. The department's inspections resulted in findings and awards to women employed at laundries, restaurants, telephone companies, basket factories, millinery establishments, retail stores, cigar factories, hotels, and candy factories. Reports of findings of commission were forwarded to the National Consumer League, among others. In her final report,[156] McCabe noted:

> The demand for the Minimum Wage and Maximum Hour Law is an expression of awakened social conscience of the people of Arkansas. Thinking men and women are everywhere realizing the individual and social menace of the low wage, and demanding that it be made possible for able-bodied, willing women to earn their living by their day's work.
>
> The right to earn a living and the right to live are indistinguishable terms. We are told that wages of women need not be adequate for their support, as many of the girls and women live at home. When this fact is given by the employer, he admits he is not paying a living wage, as the brother or father has to supply what he refuses to pay.[157]

Despite McCabe's concern, the history of women's entry into the public workplace reveals that women's working for lower salaries was already an established practice; by 1917, salary disparities were well ingrained within American society. As an example, Catherine Beecher, whose vision for improved teaching in the early 1800s influenced young women to take up the calling with missionary zeal, sold the idea of female teachers to school boards by reminding them that women did not need as much salary as men.[158]

McCabe's concern referred to the department's findings for women working in mostly non-unionized, predominately female-staffed commercial entities. That scenario provides a striking contrast to working men's concerns that women, who were willing to work for lesser wages, would lower the threshold of salaries for men when they returned after the war.

Although women were urged to accept their patriotic duty by filling vacated positions, they were sometimes greeted with disdain. In fact, fifteen yard clerks quit their jobs because nine women had been hired to labor alongside them at the Missouri Pacific Railroad's Fort Smith Crossing in North Little Rock. The men reportedly told their general manager that they were afraid the women might hear objectionable language.[159] These nine women were hired into traditionally male positions—which could have been a step forward for women; however, the "cold statistics in government reports…[demonstrate that] the vast majority" of women hired by the railroad companies were concentrated in "the traditional female occupations."[160]

In January 1918, the general manager of the Little Rock Railway and Electric Company announced another likely first—the probability of hiring women as conductors for the city's streetcars. He anticipated "the young thing of 16, if she takes her job seriously enough, may be among the number, as well as the settled woman of 30."[161] Noting that women had been successful as conductors in Brooklyn and Cleveland, he expected candidates to spend several weeks learning the job by watching male employees. The newly hired employees would work at night as well as during the day and would receive $1.75 to $2.00 per day. Several women had already applied.[162]

Two days later—with no explanation—the company purchased a large advertisement in which it laid out its argument for hiring women as streetcar conductors. The essay, titled "No Honest Work is Derogatory to Woman," noted that many women had plowed, chopped, and picked cotton, and worked in the corn to assist father and husband. In addition, many women were dishwashers, chambermaids, and cashiers in restaurants and candy stores. Others worked in laundries, factories, and offices. All of these jobs were honest and honorable work. The essay then asked, "In what way does the work of conductor on a street car differ from all these occupations?"[163] Noting that hiring women conductors was a necessity brought on by war conditions, the piece then pointed overseas, where Russian and British women were involved in every occupation but shooting a gun, although Russian women had done that. In England—and in some American cities in which there was a greater shortage of men—women had taken the place of men in heavy, strenuous work, such as loading freight cars.[164]

The title of the Little Rock Railway and Electric Company's advertisement seemed to indicate that women—or their male family members—were the likely target of the streetcar company's missive. Conversely, the Amalgamated Association of Street and Electric Railway Employees of America, affiliated with the American Federation of Labor, had already waged a bitter anti-woman-conductor campaign nationally as streetcar managers in larger urban centers had begun to explore the possibility of recruiting women for vacancies in the car crews, an area for which women had not previously been considered.[165]

Historians have found that, through unionization, men had battled for living wages and appropriate working conditions for themselves for decades; the addition of thousands of women into the work force during the war created havoc within industries. For the most part, men's objections to women workers' entry into industrial positions had to do with their fears that women would accept lower pay and benefits, thus diluting standards of income and benefits for which men had struggled.[166]

Although men were concerned about women's accepting lower salaries as they filled traditionally male positions, during the war long-time working women in conventionally female occupations were struggling for their piece of the pie as they joined unions and even picketed against well-established industrial players. In Arkansas, strikes by Fort Smith and Little Rock telephone operators against Southwestern Bell Telephone Company attracted nationwide attention in fall 1917 as Arkansas's women engaged in public brouhahas with a major industrial player. Both labor and management took advantage of newspapers to state their cases and to attempt to garner sympathy. In Little Rock, telephone operators, who had formed a union on September 1, left their jobs on September 18. On October 7, the former employees explained the situation in an *Arkansas Ga-*

zette advertisement titled "A Statement from Discharged Telephone Operators." The women averred that the dispute was over low wages insufficient to cover even meager expenses and that employees brought in from Dallas and St. Louis, purportedly earning $50.00 monthly plus expenses, were "strikebreakers."[167] The newspaper account, which began, "We have been called 'striking telephone girls.' These are the facts[,]" included a testimonial from one of the women:

> I have been working for the telephone company for a year and a half as local operator, and the highest wage I ever received was $7.20 for a week of seven days, a day consisting of eight and nine hours. I frequently worked from half an hour to a full hour overtime but did not receive pay for this. If I was off even an hour I was docked for the loss of time.
>
> Out of my wages I had to support myself and my expenses were as follows: My board was $3.00 a week. Café bill from $2 to $3 a week. I did my own washing and ironing. After paying my room rent and my bills I had left from $1.20 to $2.20 a week with which to buy my clothes, pay street car fare and other incidentals. I could not make both ends meet and am now in debt, although I have economized in every manner possible.[168]

According to Southwestern Bell, the Little Rock walkout was the result of the company's gearing up for a massive increase in government and commercial activity as plans materialized for a national cantonment site (temporary military quarters) to be built at Camp Pike in North Little Rock. The company's own large advertisement in the local newspaper, titled "A Statement of Facts to the Public," stated that working conditions were strained by the hiring of numerous additional employees, the termination of several who did not meet the company's standards of efficiency and customer service, and the transfer in of six experienced workers from other cities on September 18. Concurrently, on September 18, ten employees left their work without explanation, and thirty-eight others did not report for duty but asked for their salary by telephone. The ad continued, saying "but some of our former employes [*sic*] have been taken in hand by persons who have appeared lately in this city and who have induced these girls to give up their positions."[169]

In Fort Smith, sixty-three operators went on strike on September 19, following the discharge from employment of two members of their union. The operators remained on strike until December 27, the day following the company's agreement with a federal arbitrator to reinstate the striking operators only. The local manager would determine the disposition of the two discharged employees, who would be allowed to appeal a negative determination to the president of the company. The federal arbitrator would remain in Fort Smith until the parties reached an agreement as to wages and hours. A December 27 newspaper article noted the strike's significance:

> The local strike has attracted nation-wide attention and has been watched with interest by labor organizations everywhere. During the early days of the walkout several near riots occurred, but luckily no blood was shed. Both the company and the striking operators refused to give any ground, the latter fact resulting in a general strike of all unions allied with the Fort Smith Trades and Labor Council.[170]

Operators of exchanges at Van Buren, Huntington, Midland, Mansfield, and Hartford—who had walked out in sympathetic strikes—returned to their jobs.[171]

The Little Rock and Fort Smith operators were not alone in their struggles. In fact, during the war years—as women took advantage of employee shortages and greatly increased opportunities to change jobs or to bargain for better conditions—operators' unions were active throughout the country. Between 1900 and 1920, the occupation had grown from 19,000 to 98,000 nationwide; during the war years, thousands of telephone operators enrolled in the International Brotherhood of Electrical Workers (IBEW). During summer 1918, the IBEW's Telephone Department prepared a circular to encourage

Chicago's 7,000 operators to organize. Excerpts from the circular provide insights into the rhetoric that likely influenced Little Rock and Fort Smith operators to become militant toward Southwestern Bell:

> Compare your wages with those of organized girls. Why should a telephone operator be rated lower than a typist or stenographer? Today a girl can walk into a factory and learn to run a punch press right off the reel and she gets more money than you make after you train for weeks and weeks and work for years....The Boston girls believe that the girl operating at the telephone exchange is rendering just as essential and patriotic service as the operator who is in government service.
>
> Does she get the same pay?...The Bureau of Labor Statistics shows that the cost of living has increased 70 percent—have your wages?[172]

As other women were hired into lucrative factory positions because of the war, long-term employees' concerns of being treated unfairly led to militant actions—even in Arkansas. In the first volume of his two-volume history of women and the American labor movement, Philip Foner noted that, in 1915, the federal Commission on Industrial Relations found that women in industry and other fields of work were exploited "to an extent which threatens their health and welfare and menaces the wage and salary standards of men."[173] The commission went on to find that they were "subject to overwork, unreasonable hours, and personal abuse of various kinds."[174] As an example, the commission presented evidence of inadequate wages and unacceptable working conditions of telephone operators in seven cities (which did not include Little Rock or Fort Smith). Wartime opportunities resulting from short supply and greater demand, however, apparently gave women workers the impetus to act on their own behalf.[175]

And yet, the war created unanticipated positive consequences as well. Just as teaching had metamorphosed from a male-dominated profession into a women's profession during the late 1800s, 1870 was the beginning of a sixty-year period in which clerical work was gradually redefined as women's work. As small, family-run companies were replaced by large enterprises with distant customers, a need emerged for workers to manage letters and files. During the same period, the invention of the typewriter coincided with a massive increase in the amount of paperwork generated by companies. Women had gradually taken over the clerical work, which had become an acceptable occupation for women; yet, almost fifty years later, there was still room for women to fill positions in the top echelon of the clerical hierarchy.[176]

In August 1918, for example, women's breakthroughs into traditionally male secretarial positions in government offices were noted in articles printed just eleven days apart in the *Arkansas Gazette*. In Little Rock, Nellie Mae Bossart, who had been a stenographer in the mayor's office, was selected to become Mayor Charles E. Taylor's private secretary after the incumbent—the mayor's son—resigned to enter the naval aviation service. Bossart would be the first female private secretary to a Little Rock mayor. Less than two weeks later, another article announced that Secretary William C. Redfield, a member of the president's cabinet, had appointed Agathe C. Stewart of Port Richmond, New York, as his private secretary. The article speculated that Stewart was likely the first woman to serve as the private secretary to a cabinet member.[177]

Chapter 7: Registering Women for Service

"You never can tell where 'twill lead to when you begin to sign things."[178]

In the AFWC section of the January 18, 1918, *Arkansas Gazette*, Lettie Dodge Gibson, president of the Arkansas Federation of Women's Clubs, chastised the state's club women for not making sure that requests for help were completely met. After reminding the women of the comfort their hand-knitted sweaters had provided for soldiers, she asked, "Do you want me to tell you the real things that we may do or would you rather we just talked about being busy for good results and let it go at that?"[179] Gibson's concern was that participation was not universal among club members and that some needs went unfulfilled. In the same newspaper, Florence King, a Chicago lawyer and president of the Woman's Association of Commerce of the United States of America, took a stance that echoed Gibson's sentiment but followed a different approach: "Wake up, women, it's war."[180] King noted that knitting was not enough and should be left to "women with children they cannot leave and to semi-invalids."[181] Instead, she encouraged women to "attend to wounded, grow food, enter business and keep the factory wheels moving."[182]

At the same time, the Arkansas Woman's Committee was finalizing plans for a registration-for-service campaign for the state's women. Members had spent time in Chicago, studying methods used in Illinois's successful endeavor. Governor Brough set aside the week of February 17–23 for the campaign; training for registrars had begun January 7. Each county's woman's committee received a training manual and other literature that explained the reasons for the campaign. African American women were trained as registrars for their campaign.[183] During the week, 75,000 posters would be distributed over the state, trained registrars would set up booths in convenient places, and house-to-house canvassing would be made when necessary.[184]

Women of all ages were urged to indicate willingness and ability to perform a variety of occupations. In Crawford County, two young women's completed cards provide insights into women's expectations and abilities to serve. Julia Wade was a twenty-six-year-old African American woman and citizen by birth of the United States. Wade resided in Van Buren, was married, and indicated that she had twelve persons who were dependent upon her. Having completed grammar school, she volunteered to work during her spare time in four of the sixty-one multiple-choice, preprinted categories: "cleaning," "cooking," "laundress," and "waitress." She would be able to work in her home town only and wrote "V.P." (likely meaning volunteer, paid) in response to three service choices: "volunteer," "expenses only," or "paid."[185]

Astelle Norfleet, on the other hand, was a single, white, nineteen-year-old woman. She was a citizen by birth of the United States, lived in Van Buren, and had completed grammar school plus one year of high school. She was presently working as a telephone operator for Southwestern Bell Telephone Company in Van Buren and gave her employer as a reference. Norfleet indicated that she could perform the following types of service: "stenography," "cleaning," "housekeeping," "waitress," and "telephone operator." Under "Social Services," she checked that she could read aloud or be a relief visitor. Like Wade, Norfleet entered "V.P." in response to the three service choices. Unlike Wade, however, she had no dependents and indicated that she could "go anywhere" at "any time."[186]

The registration cards were intended "to indicate the chief usefulness of the women of Arkansas in this crisis, to give strength to the government and mobilize the spiritual resources that did much to help prosecute this righteous war."[187] The complete report sent to Washington after the war showed that 43,000 Arkansas women registered for service, as well as reporting total numbers registered in each of 155 trades and professions. Jobs were sorted into eight broad categories, as shown here:

Number Registered	Percent of 43,000	Category
12,245	28.5	Agriculture, home gardens, apple picking, cotton picking, etc.
6,625	15.4	Clerical
32,237	75.0	Domestic
4,657	10.8	Trained for social service
3,576	8.3	Industrial
5,112	11.9	Professional
1,912	4.4	Public service, mail routes, telephone, telegraph
5,259	12.2	Red Cross work[188]

Of those who registered, 75 percent volunteered to perform domestic duties, and 28.5 percent were willing to do agricultural work. These two categories would be expected among a mostly rural, minimally educated population. However, Astelle Norfleet, who was working at the time as a telephone operator and was apparently trained in stenography, also volunteered to do cleaning, housekeeping, and waitress work. Despite Julia Wade's numerous dependents and accompanying responsibilities as a young wife, she too was willing to do her part. Wade and Norfleet's example, in addition to vignettes shared below, indicate that the women who signed the cards took the registration-for-service campaign seriously and were willing to contribute their skills as their patriotic duty.

Ten counties did not conduct a registration-for-service campaign; others reported varying degrees of success. Some counties went all out to ensure a successful outcome. In Jackson County, "during registration week, four-minute speeches were made each night at the moving picture theatres, and patriotic songs were sung."[189] On two nights a special song, titled "Register," was sung. The report continued, "A splendid lesson for those who did not register was the instance of a fine old lady who had a son in the war. The lady is totally blind, but she came to be registered, and made out a special card. She gave several hours each week to the Red Cross, made button holes and other work, and knitted between times."[190] In contrast, although

Little River County registered more than 200 women, its committee members "found the women indifferent and the men suspicious."[191]

Mountainous Stone County's report noted that the country was rough, making travel difficult except on horseback, resulting in only 300 women who registered. In Van Buren County, another isolated area, sixty-eight women registered, mostly under the domestic occupations. Mississippi County reported that its African American women had participated in the work by registering for service, signing food cards, and buying Red Cross seals. Baxter County—in an isolated area on the Missouri border—registered 273 women. In Chicot County, a mother of six children commented that she could not get away from home but would be glad to do truck gardening or canning to help the government. Clay County reported that every woman in the little town of Success registered. One woman walked a mile to the nearest station to catch the early train for Success, the nearest registering point. In Brookings, a mother of nine children, who did all her own work, offered to do anything she could for the government two days each week. Craighead County reported that fifteen women registered to assist farm women during the summer, in the farm women's homes, in canning, preserving, and cooking for harvest hands. In addition, the report noted that one African American woman, who was a college graduate and had completed post-graduate work, registered to convince fellow African American women to help the cause. Also in Craighead County,

the first to present herself at the registration booth was a woman with her oldest daughter, who had driven from four miles in the country. She said she and her husband had lived in Germany until their oldest son was five years of age. They then moved to the United States and her husband took out his first naturalization papers, but died before completing them. At the time war was declared against Germany her son wanted to enlist, but he was declared an enemy alien and was not allowed to enter the army. The mother was very much distressed for fear she and her daughter could not register. She consulted a lawyer and came back with a radiant face saying, "Oh yes, it is all right; we can register." Although she had six children at home dependent on her for support, she registered to knit for the Red Cross two hours every afternoon.[192]

Both the registrar and the German woman's reactions would not have been expected during such a difficult conflict. Throughout the nation in general—and Arkansas in particular—anti-German sentiment was pervasive. Researcher Shirley Schuette noted, however, that soon after the declaration of war, the executive committee of the German-American Federation of Arkansas, made up of more than forty local societies, passed a resolution and released it publicly: "We hereby renew our pledge of loyalty to support the government of this country and to assist in every way in our power to protect and maintain the present and future interest, honor and welfare of the people of the United States."[193] Nevertheless, Arkansans remained suspicious throughout the war; even Hamp Williams, state food administrator, had employed anti-German rhetoric and name-calling tactics as he urged Arkansans to join the food conservation campaign in fall 1917.

Although the percentage of women who refused to sign the registration-for-service cards is unknown, a few counties throughout the state gave examples of reasons for the refusals. In Pope County, 470 women registered, but some were afraid they would be forced to patrol the Mexican border, and others were sure they would be sent to France. One Pope County woman opined, "You never can tell where 'twill lead to when you begin to sign things."[194] Crawford County registered 1,000 women, but "because of German propaganda, and in some instances the lack of ability to grasp the need of registration, this work was long drawn out."[195] In Jackson County, where 997 women registered, some refused to sign because "they did not want to become converts to woman suffrage,"[196] and they were afraid they would have to leave home, husband, and children.

In Dallas County, where 612 women registered, the chairman noted that women's fear of being subject to draft by signing the cards was not valid because "the best argument used against this was that if it should ever become necessary for the united states [*sic*] to draft its women, the matter of registration or non-registration would make no difference."[197] The chairman continued, "In only three instances were there any unpatriotic expressions, and two of these merely said they did not approve of the war."[198]

The Randolph County chairman reported that many women feared that they would be "taken at once into active service as Red Cross nurses, to go along with men and fight, or to do some other unknown thing. Some of these women could scarcely read or write. When the cards were explained and they were convinced that they would not be asked to leave their homes, many of them consented to be registered."[199] Arkansas women's fears—of the unknown, the federal government, and the possibility of being swept away from family and home and sent to various distant locales—make the fact that 43,000 women actually signed the cards an even greater accomplishment for organizers.

As author J. Blake Perkins noted, "In Arkansas, particularly in the vast number of rural communities across the state, many citizens even by 1917 remained either staunchly opposed to or unconvinced and apathetic about the U.S. government's decision to involve the nation abroad in the Great War."[200] Lack of information and adequate communication, in combination with isolation from the outside world, likely added to women's prevailing suspicion and fear. In addition to highlighting the misinformation and hesitancy to participate throughout Arkansas, the registration campaign also provided a scenario in which educated, middle-class volunteers were required to interact with less-educated women with whom they had little in common. Volunteers' reactions were varied, as some—including the Randolph County chairman—reacted with no outward show of condescension or disdain while others seemed to find the responses to be implausible.[201]

Despite some women's refusals to sign, the registration-for-service campaign provided a degree of concrete help within Arkansas during the remaining months of the war. Although retired teachers were located to fill vacancies as regular teachers took higher-paying jobs and clerical help was supplied to local exemption boards, perhaps the greatest result was the placement of practical nurses at the disposal of the State Board of Health during the devastating Spanish influenza crisis in fall 1918.

The statewide success was limited, however, as shown in the Report of the Arkansas Woman's Committee:

> The State only showed a ten per cent registration, many of the registrars reporting they could not induce the women of their county to register on account of the many false rumors spread that if women registered they would be conscripted. Many men refused to permit their wives to register, and although great publicity was given to the movement, it was met with half-hearted response and grave doubts.[202]

In spite of Hamp Williams's harsh words to the state's men during the second food conservation campaign a few months earlier, husbands continued to refuse to permit their wives to participate. Although some vacancies were filled as a result of the February campaign, county woman's committees were later directed to conduct separate emphases to encourage additional women to sign up for vacated teaching positions and to volunteer to be trained as nurses.

Chapter 8: Recruiting New Teachers and Nurses

"Little River County reported that its campaign to recruit student nurses was unsuccessful because 'every girl with a high school education could obtain a position as a teacher in country schools.'"[203]

During the summer of 1918, counties again conducted registration campaigns. This time, the targeted audience was young women with high school diplomas, who would qualify as prospective teachers. Women had been teaching for some time in Arkansas, so women with high school educations could fit easily into the profession; one source even referred to retired female teachers who were willing to fill vacated positions. Archival abstracts provided by the Bureau of the Census indicate that from 1872 through 1910, the percentage of Arkansas's teaching positions filled by women increased from 22.7 to 53.2 percent. Although the number of male teachers gradually increased during the thirty-eight years, the rate of increase in the number of female teachers was significantly greater, which created the percentage gap.[204]

Arkansas's Teachers, 1872 through 1910

School year ended	Male school teachers	Percent male teachers	Female school teachers	Percent female teachers	Total no. of teachers
1872	1,400*	77.3	410*	22.7	1,810*
1882	2,044	81.7	457	18.3	2,501
1890	3,437	68.5	1,579	31.5	5,016
1900	4,099	60.9	2,628	39.1	6,727
1910	4,453	46.8	5,069	53.2	9,522

*Figures were annotated as approximate.

In fact, historians have noted that, despite women's dominance within the teaching profession during our lifetime, college-educated men were the only teachers in America's classrooms until the mid-nineteenth century. However, education reformers considered the home and school to be two "naturally feminine realms in which women could nurture the next generation."[205] And, according to historian Dana Goldstein, women had "a peculiar power of awakening the sympathies of children, and inspiring them with a desire to excel."[206] At the same time, there were "widespread nineteenth-century assumptions about women's lack of intellectual capacity,"[207] which provided a natural connection between the promotion of non-college-educated female teachers and the accepted philosophy that "public schools should focus more on developing children's character than on increasing their academic knowledge beyond basic literacy and numeracy."[208]

But that was not all. Working women, most of whom were young and single, were willing to accept lower pay. An 1842 manual for New York's schools noted that the most talented women would be willing to work for half the salary required by men of the "poorest capacity."[209] By the 1890s, according to Goldstein, "American public school teaching had developed less as a female ministry and more as a working-class job for young women barely out of adolescence."[210]

By 1890, women made up two-thirds of teachers nationwide as men left the profession for higher-paying jobs. Wealthier and more developed states experienced an even greater rate of attrition for male teachers. In Massachusetts, for example, women filled 90 percent of all teaching positions by 1890.[211] Conversely, in a poor state such as Arkansas, male teachers retained their positions for several years longer, resulting in women's filling fewer than one-third of the state's classroom teaching positions by that same year.[212]

Public schools were of major concern for Arkansas's Progressive Era leaders; high schools were all but non-existent. And as women gradually became the majority among teachers, they endured a number of discouraging factors such as the consequences of local funding, or lack thereof; an environment, particularly in rural areas, that did not value education; a paucity of centralized oversight; a mindset that condoned child labor; and a disconcerting rate of illiteracy. In fact, in 1902 there were more than 500 school districts with fewer than twenty students each. By 1912, there were still 5,143 districts. In 1910 the few high schools in the state graduated only 300 students, and just a small portion of high school teachers had more than an eighth-grade education.[213]

County teacher recruitment activity reports during the summer 1918 campaign included one from Faulkner County, which published articles in county newspapers "urging those who were capable of teaching school to enter the profession at once, as a patriotic duty, so that vacancies left by men entering military service might be filled at once."[214] Crawford County furnished a report to headquarters of all women who registered as being qualified as teachers. Little River County reported that its campaign to recruit student nurses was unsuccessful because "every girl with a high school education could obtain a position as a teacher in country schools."[215] Polk County proudly noted that "in regard to our women responding to the call for teachers, we are proud to report that all our teachers in Mena are women, even in the High School, and they are having great success."[216]

The Polk County report indicated that high school teaching positions had previously been filled primarily by men. Statistical data indicate that Polk County's figures were consistent with those of school districts throughout the state. Although women filled 53.2 percent of all public school teaching positions in 1910, they held only 40 percent of positions in high schools. The war, however, provided increased opportunities for women to teach in high schools, as indicated by an increase from 46 percent in 1915 to 61.8 percent by June 1918.[217] However, the so-called "opportunity" was perhaps a mixed blessing. In fact, it is likely that Goldstein accurately described teaching in Arkansas's high schools when she stated that "during the Progressive Era, it was working-class female teachers who were attacked [by school reformers], for lacking the masculine 'starch' supposedly necessary to preside over sixty-student classrooms of former child laborers."[218]

The Need for Nurses Escalates

Early in the war, the need for Red Cross workers overseas led to stateside training camps for women. In Searcy, seventy-nine women began military training, naming their group "Brough's Guards," with instruction provided by the recruiting officer for the Third Regiment. The women were expected to take up Red Cross work following their training.[219] At Hardy, a two-week military training camp for women and girls from Arkansas, Mississippi, and Tennessee gave instruction in military, hospital, and Red Cross work. Trainees attended classes in fever nursing, dietetics, bacteriology, anatomy, home nursing, surgical dressing, first aid, life-saving, battalion drill, setting-up drill, and target practice. Upon completion, they received certificates enabling them to volunteer to the government for Red Cross work. Although the training was brief and intense, courses of instruction indicate that graduates would be eligible for overseas duty, likely in military hospitals.[220]

By November 1917, newspaper coverage had turned to the need for trained nurses. From Washington came word that the medical department of the U.S. Army had begun a campaign to immediately enlist 500 graduate nurses in the Army Nurse Corps. Selectees would be assigned to duty at base hospitals at army and National Guard divisional cantonments, where they would be paid $50 a month and maintenance.[221] The Red Cross projected that 20,000 trained nurses would be called up to serve in military hospitals in the United States and Europe. Because the vast majority of qualified nurses would be called on to serve through either the U.S. military or the American Red Cross military nurse corps, Arkansas was left without an adequate number of nurses. The child conservation department worked to ensure adequate numbers of public health nurses, provide classes in home nursing and dietetics, and circulate pamphlets on "First Aid to the Injured," which were sent to mothers throughout Arkansas.[222] Local Red Cross chapters geared up training schedules in order to teach women the rudiments of nursing so that they could meet emergencies in their own homes. Courses in elementary hygiene, home care of the sick, dietetics, and first aid would be offered.[223]

As shortages of military nurses became critical in 1918, the state chairman of the registration department coordinated a student nurse drive, which resulted in 209 student nurses recruited and sent throughout the United States for training. Although some counties failed to recruit any student nurses, the 209 recruits made up slightly more than 50 percent of Arkansas's quota of 400, which was comparable to the percentage of student nurses recruited nationwide. As an example, Miller County reported registration of one Red Cross nurse, twelve graduate nurses, five student nurses, six African American practical nurses, and two white practical nurses. Although most individual counties' reports did not mention two registrations, Polk County clarified that there were two separate nurse recruitment campaigns: first, a July 1918 campaign in which young women were called on to volunteer for the U.S. Student Nurse Reserve and, second, an additional registration for the Army School of Nursing.[224]

Several counties indicated seemingly enthusiastic responses to the call for nurse trainees. However, Pulaski County's report noted, "In the call for student nurses, 30 applicants were accepted. The lack of sufficient education was most distressing, and the slacking of those who had the education almost more so."[225] Because the final reports were submitted during December 1918, several counties mentioned that women who signed up during registration-for-service campaigns were recruited a few months later to provide assistance as the Spanish influenza epidemic ravaged Arkansas during September, October, and November.[226]

The dire need for trained nurses during the war was a testament to the success of the nursing profession's extended struggle for recognition and regulation. Historians have found that in the mid-nineteenth century, those who worked in hospitals were neither esteemed nor subject to much regulation. Hospital workers, who were, according to Philip Foner, "looked down upon by their society and their times…were forced to work in institutions under the most miserable conditions."[227] In early hospitals, mostly uneducated women cared for sick female patients, while men attended to male patients.[228]

In the decades following 1873, the year in which nurses' training was introduced within the United States, trained nurses in various states pursued registration, or licensing, as they sought the same legal protections as those attained by physicians. Arkansas's nurses followed suit, and in 1913, Act 128, the Arkansas Nurse Practice Act, was passed by the state legislature. For Arkansas's trained nurses, the act signified a victory for professional nurses as it underscored their claim that the care of the sick was best performed by those who were specifically trained for that purpose.[229]

During fall 1917, provisions of Act 128 were carried out in the Senate chamber of the Arkansas State Capitol as fifty candidates went before the nursing board of examiners in order to be registered as trained nurses. All nurses' training schools in the state were represented at the two-day examinations. Frankie Hutchinson, secretary of the board of examiners, was in charge of the proceedings.[230] Six days later, she was re-elected president of the state nursing association at its annual meeting, during which members voted to increase trained nurses' salaries to $5.00 daily because of the high cost of living.[231]

The first nurses' training school in Arkansas was established at St. John's Hospital in Fort Smith; in 1898, three students graduated. A survey in 1914 found sixteen schools, each with three to forty-five students. In most cases, students made up the entire nursing staff of the training hospital, with one graduate nurse as superintendent.[232] Three trained nurses, all of whom were likely products of Arkansas's nurse training schools, serve as examples of Arkansas's registered nurses who were stationed stateside as well as overseas during the war.

First was Helen K. Blacknall, who was born in Arkansas in 1886 and listed her home address as Helena. Blacknall was called into active service as a nurse on November 22, 1917, and was returned from active duty status to reserve status on May 17, 1919. Blacknall served in various hospitals, including an overseas tour from September 24, 1918, to April 6, 1919.[233]

The second Arkansas nurse was Eva Atwood, who was born in Malvern in 1890 and returned to Springdale after her service. Atwood was called into active service as a nurse on November 30, 1917. She served in various hospitals, including an overseas tour that lasted almost nine months, from September 28, 1918, to June 19, 1919. She was honorably returned to reserve nurse status in June 1919.[234]

Allie R. Bennett, the third Arkansas native, was born in Benton and listed Benton as her home. Bennett was born on August 2, 1878, and was called into active service on March 15, 1918. She spent her entire tour at the base hospital at Camp Pike, Arkansas, and was honorably returned to reserve status on January 13, 1919, having completed ten months of service. The discharge document for each of the three indicated no engagements, wounds, or disabilities incurred. All three nurses were white.[235]

Although nurses at Camp Pike were likely from various regions of the United States, photographs of the nurses and facilities at Camp Pike are especially meaningful because some nurses stationed there—including Allie R. Bennett—were Arkansas women.

The Woman's Committee of the Council of Defense for Arkansas, July 1, 1917, to December 30, 1918. *(Arkansas State Archives)*

Ida Frauenthal, chairman of the Woman's Committee, was the only female member of the Council of Defense for Arkansas. *(Arkansas State Archives)*

Women led the way in a Liberty Loan parade in Van Buren. The Arkansas Woman's Committee sold 26,859 bonds worth $7,848,750, mostly through door-to-door canvassing. *(UALR Center for Arkansas History and Culture)*

Home demonstration agents (shown here in 1919) played a pivotal role during the war as they helped women to can and prepare meals despite shortages. *(Special Collections, University of Arkansas)*

The first home demonstration work began in Mabelvale in 1912 with this group of girls in a tomato club. Their mothers soon followed suit. *(Special Collections, University of Arkansas)*

Safe canning was vital to the wartime program of thrift in the kitchen. The first canning demonstration in 1912 was a family affair. *(Special Collections, University of Arkansas)*

The home demonstration work helped rural women and their neighbors survive during the economic depressions of the 1920s and 1930s. This canning session was in 1929. *(Special Collections, University of Arkansas)*

Red Cross canteen volunteers in Van Buren await the troop train with sandwiches and coffee. *(UALR Center for Arkansas History and Culture)*

Soldiers from a troop train take a break at the Van Buren railroad station. *(UALR Center for Arkansas History and Culture)*

Red Cross nursing class at Leslie, Arkansas. The young women were likely training for overseas Red Cross work. *(Arkansas State Archives)*

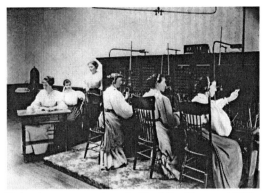

Telephone operators in Fort Smith, ca. 1900. In 1917, operators in Fort Smith and Little Rock went on strike against Southwestern Bell. *(UALR Center for Arkansas History and Culture)*

Red Cross nurse Maude Hines of Pulaski County was the great-aunt of Carla Hines Coleman, longtime member of the Arkansas Black History Commission. *(Arkansas State Archives)*

The Ladies Exchange in Little Rock had a Red Cross sticker in its window. According to an archival description, the store seems to have provided an outlet for women to sell their home-produced wares to other women. *(UALR Center for Arkansas History and Culture)*

Fifteen yard workers walked off their jobs at the Fort Smith Crossing in North Little Rock when nine women were hired to labor alongside them in January 1918. *(North Little Rock History Commission)*

A secretary works in her office in about 1912. The war created opportunities for women to move up to private secretary positions. *(UALR Center for Arkansas History and Culture)*

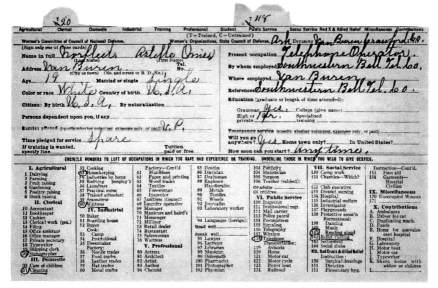

Registration-for-Service card signed by Astelle Norfleet of Van Buren during the statewide campaign in February 1918. *(Arkansas State Archives)*

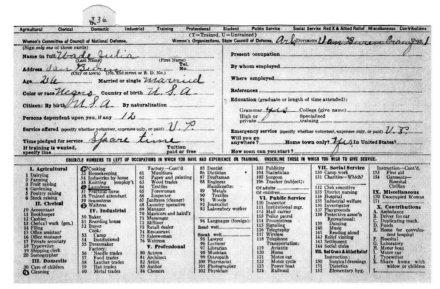

Registration-for-Service card signed by Julia Wade of Van Buren during the statewide campaign in February 1918. *(Arkansas State Archives)*

German Lutheran Church, Fort Smith, Ark.

German families were already well established in Arkansas. This German Lutheran Church in Fort Smith was photographed in about 1910. *(UALR Center for Arkansas History and Culture)*

Four German adults stand in front of their store on West 12th Street in Little Rock. Germans in Arkansas were regarded with suspicion during the war. *(UALR Center for Arkansas History and Culture)*

These student nurses in 1916 were part of a struggle by trained nurses to be recognized professionally. *(Arkansas State Archives)*

Outside view of nurses' quarters at Camp Pike. *(Butler Center for Arkansas Studies, Central Arkansas Library System)*

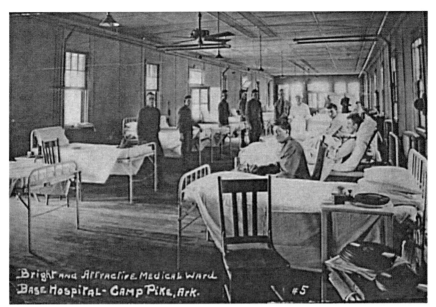

Nurses on duty in the Camp Pike base hospital medical unit. *(National Guard Museum, Camp Robinson, Arkansas)*

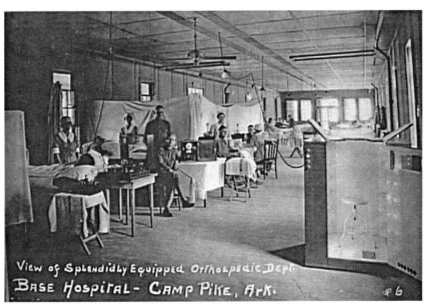

Nurses on duty in the "splendidly equipped orthopedic department" of the Camp Pike base hospital. *(National Guard Museum, Camp Robinson, Arkansas)*

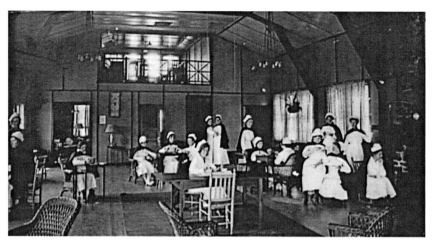

Trained, registered nurses were in great demand during the war. These Camp Pike nurses likely include some Arkansas nurses. *(Butler Center for Arkansas Studies)*

The national YWCA provided funding for the lovely Hostess House for female family members of soldiers at Camp Pike. *(Butler Center for Arkansas Studies)*

Another view of the Hostess House, which was near the Camp Pike Missouri Pacific Station. *(National Guard Museum, Camp Robinson, Arkansas)*

The beautiful interior of the YWCA Hostess House, staffed by employees and volunteers of the Little Rock YWCA. *(National Guard Museum, Camp Robinson, Arkansas)*

By 1920, the Hostess House had been renovated into a college facility. *(National Guard Museum, Camp Robinson, Arkansas)*

Roland, Arkansas, school photograph, 1917. Arkansas's women worked to make schools better during the war with little success. *(Arkansas State Archives)*

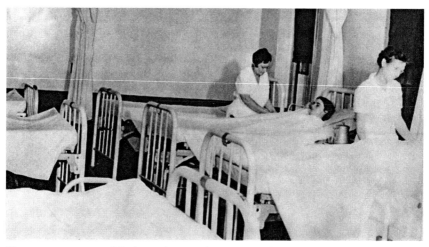

These women provided nursing assistance to University of Arkansas students during the Spanish influenza epidemic in fall 1918. *(Special Collections, University of Arkansas)*

The Center Ridge school's 1917 photograph seems to show several older children in school—a rarity in Arkansas until the late 1910s. *(Arkansas State Archives)*

Arkansas's women suffragists (shown here with Governor Charles H. Brough) suspended most of their political work during the war in order to do their "bit" for the "boys." *(Arkansas State Archives)*

Chapter 9: Fearing the Worst for the Cantonment City

"If the morality of the home was to be protected from outside forces which threatened it, then those who stood for that morality must go outside the home."[236]

In its first meeting, on July 2, 1917, the Arkansas Woman's Committee appointed two women to confer with a representative of the army camp entertainment committee and with Governor Charles H. Brough, "in an effort to protect the boys of the camp and the girls of the town and state from prostitution."[237] The cantonment cities of Little Rock and North Little Rock were of paramount concern as plans were made and carried out to build Camp Pike just west of North Little Rock. As in other areas of national concern, the federal government took tight control in protecting military camps; in this situation, its efforts were carried out through its Commission on Training Camp Activities, with Raymond B. Fosdick as director. In a letter to each state's governor and council of defense, Secretary of War Newton Baker laid responsibility for success on the state councils of defense, as "an integral part of the war machinery,"[238] writing: "The War Department intends to do its full part in these matters, but we expect the cooperation and support of the local communities. If the desired end cannot otherwise be achieved, I propose to move the camps from those neighborhoods in which clean conditions cannot be secured."[239] In a speech to women war workers in Washington DC in September 1917, Baker, noting the old stories of soldiers' camps, with their perils, disasters, and temptations, commented:

We have determined to surround our army, not with a system of prohibitions and restraints, but with a system of wholesome environments and stimulating inducements to self-improvement and high conduct, of such character that everybody who visits one of our camps will come away thrilled with the thought that at last this sort of business can be carried on in a manner highly creditable to a great nation.[240]

Further, in "the doughboy-worshiping hysteria of World War I America,"[241] as one historian described the era, there would be no let-up in attempts by the federal government and local citizens to abate prostitution and inappropriate socialization among young women and soldiers. During the war years, the federal government, the military, the Council of Defense for Arkansas, the Arkansas Woman's Committee, and other groups shared a common concern: the rampant spread of venereal disease. Nationally, the so-called "American Plan," an anti-venereal-disease provision of the war years, authorized the military to arrest any unaccompanied woman within five miles of a military cantonment and allow her arrest and detention without trial, i.e., with suspension of her civil rights.[242]

By early summer 1917, Little Rock's citizens would have only a few months in which to prepare before Camp Pike—with its population of up to 50,000 soldiers—became a reality. During the earliest months of the war, Little Rock's Social Service Club—with the Reverend R. B. Thompson, dean of Trinity Cathedral, as president and several women as officers—geared up to provide wholesome entertainment for soldiers stationed in the city. At a June 1 meeting, members were assured that providing recreation and amusement for soldiers would be Little Rock citizens' patriotic duty, in order to "turn their minds from bad and vicious influences."[243] Thompson continued by telling matrons that they should not stay away from planned activities "just because they may object to associating with a number of men who may be a bit wayward."[244]

On June 2, the committee on social affairs of the Federation of Camp Activities sponsored its first dance at the Hotel Marion in honor of men attending officers' training camp at Fort Roots as well as officers of the First Arkansas Regiment, which had just begun intensive military training "in a field between Argenta and Levy."[245]

Central Arkansas's leading ladies—including Anne Brough, wife of Arkansas's governor, and Leonora England, wife of the Arkansas adjutant general—were on the list of chaperones for the event. Each chaperone received instructions to bring one or more young women to meet the officers. The chairman of the event noted that young society girls of Little Rock should consider it their duty to attend the dance. On the following night, a dance was held for enlisted men of the First Arkansas Regiment. Each event was tightly chaperoned. During the same period, the federation launched a "take-a-soldier-home-to-dinner" campaign for soldiers who attended church services each Sunday morning.[246] Although the Arkansas Woman's Committee, as well as other women's organizations, cooperated in all activities of hospitality toward the military, the women of the state were asked to do even more.

The National Woman's Committee was asked to cooperate fully with the Commission on Training Camp Activities, and each state chairman was directed to appoint a member to represent her in this endeavor. In addition to various organizations authorized to work within and outside the camps in providing leisure-time activities for the soldiers—namely, the Young Men's Christian Association (YMCA), Knights of Columbus, and libraries, theaters, athletic groups, and music ensembles—there would be two others "of special interest, which consider in their plans the care of girls."[247] These were the subcommittee on protective work for girls and the subcommittee on proper chaperonage of girls, which were in charge of the Hostess Houses at the camps. Arkansas women's main thrust would be to work to carry out the goals of the two subcommittees.[248]

As the Council of Defense for Arkansas cooperated with the military in attempting to keep young soldiers away from prostitutes, the state Woman's Committee thus turned its attention to local young women and schoolgirls. Before the end of summer, the committee asked the *Arkansas Gazette* to republish, on its Sunday AFWC page, an editorial already printed a few days previously in another section of the newspaper. The editorial, written by Fosdick and titled "The

Flapper," discussed a problem with which women in central Arkansas were dealing:

> There are, of course, many problems which are sure to arise with the locating of a camp at any point. One of those which has already come to our attention is the flapper problem. There are a great many young girls who must be taken care of in these communities. They are carried away with admiration for the soldiers. It sometimes seems that they become hysterical at the very sight of a brass button. They are really innocent girls and very young, but it must be remembered that the soldiers are young also. We shall ask the communities in which the camps are located to cooperate with us in looking after these girls.
>
> The flapper is the leggy little lady, not yet a woman and no longer a child, who is afflicted with manitis. If you have a little flapper in your home, mother, watch her carefully. Carefully watched and trained, she should become a fine and useful woman.[249]

Although Fosdick's criticism was scathing toward young women and teenage girls, the Arkansas Woman's Committee indicated agreement with its indictment, as its members asked for a reprint on the woman's page.

One month later, representatives of thirty-five central Arkansas organizations, including the Board of Commerce, Ministerial Alliance, women's clubs, and church groups, met in the gymnasium of the Young Women's Christian Association (YWCA) to form the Health and Recreation Association. All officers and committee chairs for the new organization were women, who were appointed to head up committees on chaperones, curfew, city mothers, and mass meeting. The committee on chaperones also named presidents of all school improvement associations as members. During the meeting, the Reverend J. D. Hammons commented that at Ministerial Alliance meetings, businessmen had expressed disapproval of the clothing in which many women appeared on the streets. Hammons also assured the representatives that they would have the cooperation of the Little Rock police department.[250]

In response, Annie Griffey, primary supervisor of the Little Rock schools, led a discussion on "chaperonage," which would be the primary work of the association. Griffey spoke of the crowded conditions of the city schools as evidence of the great influx of new residents to the area. Emphasizing that each mother must take responsibility to protect her own daughter, she discussed the need for chaperones to accompany girls after six p.m. and while riding in automobiles, and to keep them off the streets on Sunday afternoons. Griffey noted that not too long ago, "there was a sentiment in Little Rock against allowing a group of young girls to go laughing and chatting down Main Street, unchaperoned, on Sunday afternoons. Now, often, young girls from some of the best homes may be seen on the street unchaperoned on Sunday afternoon."[251] As the discussion continued, the women talked about the need for a curfew—not as a law but as "an expression of sentiment"[252] because it was "bad form"[253] for young girls to be out alone after the streetlights were on.[254]

The meeting and comments were based on instructions directly from Washington, which had warned women that the "greatest of all problems that confront the women in the vicinity of the camps is that of guarding the young girl. Where soldiers are stationed either temporarily or permanently, the problem of preventing girls from being misled by the glamour and romance of war and beguiling uniforms looms large."[255] Just as other activities of the Arkansas Woman's Committee were micro-managed from Washington, so were the committee's contributions to the health and recreation work.

Although central Arkansas women's actions were controlled by the federal government, historians have noted that those actions were consistent with club women's own agendas as providers of moral strength to the family. Carry Nation, the flamboyant crusader for the temperance movement, averred that, although a woman's place may be in the home, home is wherever our loved ones are, and "a woman would be either selfish or cowardly"[256] if she refused to leave

104

her home to relieve suffering or trouble. And, "if the morality of the home was to be protected from outside forces which threatened it, then those who stood for that morality must go outside the home to ensure that their morality prevailed in the world at large."[257]

Within the separate-spheres theory that prevailed, women thus cited their moral obligations to home and community to exempt them from their accepted place in the home. "Many women in the nineteenth century felt quite comfortable being active in the world of Social Purity or temperance," one historian commented, "but would not have been caught dead working for suffrage or any other cause that directly challenged the doctrine of separate spheres, though both activities, of course, brought women 'out of the home.'"[258] Arkansas's women acted in concert with those Washington overseers and were well qualified to take on the work of the Health and Recreation Association.

Chapter 10: Performing Yeoman Duties for the City

"After the declaration of war, and the beginning of the great demand for Red Cross workers, young girls came to the city without funds, friends, or knowledge of what the work meant."[259]

In Little Rock, the Young Women's Christian Association (YWCA)—under the supervision of its national office—confronted the challenges of a cantonment city as its employees and volunteers labored to protect, comfort, and guide women of all ages who came to central Arkansas "in search of jobs, to be with their loved ones in military service, or for less laudatory purposes."[260] In her annual report for calendar year 1917, General Secretary May F. Conway noted that, beginning in August, the army situation and the constant stream of young women into the city "brought a realization of war's effect upon the womanhood of the Nation."[261] The YWCA's workload thus expanded greatly to encompass wartime-related Red Cross classes and increased women's lodging requirements, in addition to its continuing religious, social, educational, and recreational activities.

Perhaps the organization's greatest and most difficult responsibility, however, was aiding the thousands of women and girls who came by railroad to the city. According to the General Secretary's report, although many of the travelers had come to visit soldiers at Camp Pike, others thronged the city in search of jobs:

After the declaration of war, and the beginning of the great demand for Red Cross workers, young girls came to the city without funds, friends, or knowledge of what the work meant. It was our duty to send those who could not secure employment back to their homes. A number of girls who could do other work were placed in desirable positions and are now self-reliant and independent.[262]

Four travelers' aid matrons, who had police authority, were on duty at two railroad stations—as they had been during the previous six years. The matrons were on eight-hour shifts, twenty-four hours a day. The General Secretary's report for 1917 noted that the number of individuals aided had increased dramatically from the number in 1916. Realizing the great need, the Red Cross chose to pay the salaries for two additional matrons to serve at the Iron Mountain and Rock Island stations, beginning March 1, 1918. The six matrons' salaries were paid by contributions from the city of Little Rock, the YWCA Board of Directors, the Red Cross, the Rock Island and Missouri Pacific railroads, and several local churches.[263]

Although the matrons provided assistance to all travelers, the report was limited to the girls, young women, and women with children whom they aided. The 1917 report, which was printed in the weekly *Y.W.C.A. News*, noted the matrons' assistance after assessing the needs of young women, women with children, and girls whom they encountered at Little Rock's railroad stations:

Travelers' Aid Secretary's Report for Year 1917

Number	Classification of Need/Assistance
2,746	Girls traveling alone assisted
909	Girls staying over night in station
3,150	Women and children staying over night in station
2,832	Women and children staying part of night in station
1,071	Women and children traveling alone cared for
475	Girls and young women accompanied to transfer point or other station
1,543	Girls and young women accompanied or directed to hotels
137	Girls and young women accompanied to YWCA
125	Girls and young women protected from the attentions of strangers
417	Girls or children put on train in care of auditor
11	Insane cared for
266	Sick cared for
68	Sent to United Charities
331	Friends were located for
32	Positions were secured for
1,391	Local telephone calls made

110	Long distance telephone calls made
26	Inefficient unemployed persuaded to return home
14	Accompanied or sent to police station
15,654	Total[264]

The number of unaccompanied women and girls who traveled to Little Rock by railroad provides some sense of the magnitude of their impact on central Arkansas during the war.

The Little Rock YWCA was established in 1911, and its goal was to provide women and girls in the community access to education, recreation, employment, and lodging.[265] However, as Little Rock became a cantonment city, the YWCA's responsibilities grew exponentially. While the Red Cross, Arkansas Woman's Committee, and various women's organizations made other significant contributions to the war effort, the Little Rock YWCA was out in the trenches, laboring despite what appears to have been an almost insurmountable task.

In September 1917, the YWCA War Work Council of Little Rock sent its initial request to its national office for the establishment of a Hostess House at the newly built Camp Pike.[266] By December, the house had been dedicated and the assigned YWCA employees and volunteers from local women's organizations were providing comfort and guidance to hundreds of women visiting loved ones at the military post. The lovely house, which was officially presented to a representative of Camp Pike's commanding officer in an opening ceremony in December 1917, was the only building within Camp Pike's perimeter where mothers, sisters, wives, and female friends of soldiers could find a place to rest, eat lunch, and read while waiting for the men to come off duty.[267]

The house's interior was attractive and home-like, and the huge living room, in blue and amber, had a large open fireplace, numerous wicker chairs and settees, and a long reading table with beautiful lamps. Small writing tables were scattered throughout. The staff of four secretaries, i.e., administrators, stayed overnight in the house, which included four small bedrooms for them. The building was open at all times. The house, at the corner of South Avenue and Seventh Street, was the first building one saw when coming down the steps from the Camp Pike Missouri Pacific station and was close to the main automobile road. No overnight accommodations were furnished, but the ladies' rest room had cots where women could have a rest hour during the afternoon. Red Cross nurses at the base hospital were able to come to the house for recreation, rest, reading, luncheons, and a warm welcome.[268]

Although the description of the Hostess House provides a sense of calm and security, the YWCA's weekly newspaper included articles that gave a picture of frenetic activity in service to women. During the Christmas holidays of 1917, the YWCA was called upon to aid a large number of soldiers' wives who had come to Little Rock and had applied for all sorts of work. As an employment agency, the organization's largest order was a request from Western Union Telegraph Company for twenty-five messenger girls. Religious work was ongoing with employees of the Kress department store and detainees in the local jail. The newspaper's Christmas issue, which thanked the city hospital, detention home, police authorities, home service department of civilian relief of the American Red Cross, and Drs. Ogden and Harris, provides insight into "the spirit of *nobless[e] oblige* and Christian compassion"[269] in which staffers and volunteers were engaged during the preceding year.[270]

As in other areas in which Arkansas's women made significant contributions during the war, two facts remain: one, YWCA volunteers were carrying out the types of work in which they had been involved throughout the relatively new century, and, two, they were following orders directly from Washington.

Chapter 11: Making Things Better for the Children

"The least a democratic nation can do, which sends men into war, is to give a solemn assurance that their families will be cared for—not kept from starvation but kept on a wholesome level of comfort."[271]

The child welfare department of the Arkansas Woman's Committee embodied the national committee's accepted purpose—to safeguard the moral and spiritual forces of the nation "so that those inner defenses of our national life may not be broken down in the period of the war."[272] As Ida Clyde Clarke noted in her 1918 evaluation of American women's contributions to the war effort,

it did not take a declaration of war to bring the Government of the United States to a realization of the importance of caring for the moral and physical welfare of its children, nor did it take a declaration of war to direct the attention of women to this work, much of the responsibility of which naturally fell on their shoulders.[273]

Just as Clarke reported, even before the United States entered the war, the Department of Labor had created its Children's Bureau, with Julia Lathrop of Illinois as chief. The Children's Bureau was instituted during a period in which the United States had the eleventh-highest infant mortality rate in the world. Mothers worried about getting their toddlers through the second summer of the war during a time when clean milk was not universally available and most children experienced the loss of a brother or sister. Diseases caused by inadequate diets included weaning diarrhea, which was often fatal and resulted from protein malnutrition in children taken off breast milk and placed on amino-acid-deficient foods. As the newly created National Woman's Committee's child welfare department incorporated and expanded the goals and activities already begun by the Department of Labor, Lathrop became its executive chairman.[274] Delineating the overall goal for the work with children, Lathrop had noted that "the least a democratic nation can do, which sends men into war, is to give a solemn assurance that their families will be cared for—not kept from starvation but kept on a wholesome level of comfort."[275]

The wartime child welfare work was divided into two categories: first, preschool children and babies' health and well-being, and second, improvement of school children's education and school attendance. When the Children's Bureau in Washington suggested a Children's Year emphasis, March 1918 through March 1919, the Arkansas Woman's Committee's child welfare department chose representatives of various statewide organizations to serve as the state committee. Soon after, the committee learned that of 300,000 babies' lives projected to be saved during Children's Year, Arkansas's quota was 2,170.[276]

As with most Progressive Era programs instigated during the war by agencies in Washington DC, child welfare work was not new to Arkansas's women. During the decade before the war, the AFWC embraced nationally sponsored Baby Week events and baby health contests, which spotlighted children's health and eventually led to its child welfare department. The AFWC supported professionalization in the health industry and encouraged health-related legislation, including a bill to control the unregulated practice of midwifery.[277] During the Progressive Era, Arkansas made strides on health issues, although state health officials were not given complete control over health matters. In 1913, the legislature created a state board of health. Before 1920, the board carried out health initiatives backed by the federal government or private entities; it also developed plans for improved health throughout Arkansas. Hookworm was virtually eliminated with the Rockefeller Foundation's funding, and malaria was targeted through mosquito control. By the 1920s, the board turned to a program to improve the health of infants and mothers with funding from the federal government under the Sheppard-Towner Maternity and Infancy Act.[278] Through the program, the infant death rate declined and life expectancy increased throughout Arkansas.[279]

Throughout the South, a public health movement gradually took shape, but among all southern states, Arkansas was the last to establish its board of health. Southern states' efforts were supported by "charity organizations, social workers, labor unions, civic groups, and many doctors and nurses"[280] and were the result of a combination of "the diffused efforts of social reformers and pressure groups."[281] These boards tackled uniform licensing standards for doctors, nurses, and pharmacists. They set up food and milk inspections, enacted pure-food and -drug laws, and "eventually required the medical examination of school children."[282] These boards also established bureaus of vital statistics, such as Arkansas established in 1914. Women's efforts to document children's dates of birth during the war were part of this emphasis.[283]

As the state child conservation department geared up to follow its marching orders from Washington, it sent out to county organizations information concerning prenatal care, birth registration, infant feeding, and food for children. Next were campaigns to weigh and measure children younger than six years of age. By December of 1918, over 9,000 measurement cards had been returned, and the chairman expected an additional 9,000 to be reported to the Children's Bureau by April 1919—the month following the end of the campaign. The state Children's Year committee, as well as the Arkansas Public Health Association, also attempted to make the general public aware of the need for public health nurses and programs to save the lives of children.[284]

In northwestern Arkansas, the Washington County Woman's Committee submitted an especially detailed account of its activities. In fact, the committee organized a cadre of professional entities, including the Home Economics and Extension departments of the College of Agriculture, University of Arkansas; the State Public Health Association; and the city hospital. Local physicians, nurses, and volunteers also cooperated with the county's child welfare department. The work included health exhibits and lectures on the care of children, child nutrition, and social and moral conditions. Many towns in the county waged campaigns to have every child under six weighed and measured, and local committees encouraged the registration of babies through the distribution of so-called "window cards." Other efforts included the distribution of posters and exhibits in rural schools and steps to establish free clinics and to secure a visiting nurse. Washington County's report noted that the committee was particularly active among African American women as provisions were made for weighing and measuring the children and for giving instructions to the parents. The county's woman's committee also reported that its members had arranged for public meetings in which addresses were made on food conservation, War Savings Stamps, Red Cross work, health, and child welfare. [285]

Other counties reported programs customized to meet their children's needs. Bradley County's committee submitted newspaper articles titled "Food for Babies," "How to Bathe the Baby," and "How to Prevent Croup," as well as a scale of correct weights for babies. Columbia, Craighead, Crawford, Drew, and Miller counties, combined, reported weighing and measuring more than 5,000 babies and preschoolers. Miller County's report noted that birth certificates were issued to 487 white children and 200 African American children in Texarkana; in rural districts, the numbers were 277 and 248, respectively. Many counties did not elaborate on their child conservation work, and the state chairman's summary report was scanty. Most of the work was proactive, and results of the women's efforts were not known at the time reports were submitted.[286]

As the war ended and the Arkansas Woman's Committee's work was done, the home demonstration agents of Arkansas's Cooperative Extension Service, a Progressive Era program, continued into the 1920s and beyond to work diligently with school teachers and principals to improve children's health. Agents were particularly focused on weighing children, providing more nutritious options for lunch baskets, and encouraging children to drink adequate amounts of milk daily.[287]

Chapter 12: Trying to Help the Schools

"If every child released from work can be sent, well nourished and decently clothed, to a good school, under a good teacher, then the full benefit of the Federal Child Labor law will be reaped for the country's children."[288]

The second focus for each county's child conservation department was school-aged children's education and school attendance. The problem of schools and school attendance, however, was not a new concern. At the turn of the century, the improvement of Arkansas's schools may have been one of the state's most important challenges. Although agricultural prospects were not promising, opportunities in cities and in other states were possible only with adequate education. Every local school district, however, financed and controlled its own schools. In 1902, the state superintendent of public instruction criticized the fragmentation of the state's program and asked for at least the unification of county schools under a common supervisor. Using a Progressive Era analogy, he compared a school district to a business, which could not function without a head.

The themes of concentration and centralization continued throughout the Progressive Era years. The state teachers' association asked for state and private commissions to analyze school problems and offer solutions. In 1908, the Arkansas Education Commission was created; its 1911 report laid out a plan to strengthen public education, including consolidation of school districts, compulsory school attendance, and greater financial aid for high schools.[289]

Lack of centralization was only one problem for Arkansas's schools, which suffered for years from students' absenteeism, often as a result of older children working instead of attending school. In 1900, only 20 percent of children and young people aged five to twenty attended school for more than three months during a year. In 1910, the state's seventy-six accredited high schools produced only 300 graduates. Child labor was a major factor in these educational weaknesses. In 1900, one third of children ages ten to fifteen were employed—mostly in agriculture. By 1910, the total had increased to over 40 percent. These figures do not include many more children who worked for no pay at their families' farms or businesses.[290]

As might be expected, the Arkansas Federation of Women's Clubs had been active in efforts to improve Arkansas's schools and school attendance since the 1890s. In 1908, Mrs. R. B. Willis, state president, noted that the AFWC had to support the state's education "until there is not left...a single untaught, neglected child."[291] In their attempts to improve the situation, members of the AFWC founded kindergartens and libraries, and supported state laws intended to remedy the problems of school attendance and child labor.[292] The AFWC created a special committee on child labor and, in 1913, pledged to work with the Arkansas Child Labor Commission to pass a uniform child labor bill. Although the state's first significant child labor bill went into effect in 1915, house representatives immediately sabotaged the legislation by introducing bills to exempt their own counties.[293]

The employment of children had increased during "the hard times of the 1890s."[294] In 1900, an estimated 25 percent of employees in southern cotton mills were between ten and sixteen years of age. Working long hours for low wages, these children suffered from illiteracy at a rate three or four times that of other children in the same state.[295] After 1903, the sporadic efforts of state child labor reformers gradually melded into an organized, regional movement under the authority of the National Child Labor Committee.[296]

After war was declared, the Council of National Defense joined the U.S. Department of Education in its efforts to make childhood education a priority through its Children's Year program. Arkansas's women were tasked with the dual responsibility of working toward improved education as well as improved school attendance. The loss of teachers to the military as well as to higher-paying positions was an obvious by-product of the war. However, problems of poverty, illiteracy, malnutrition, lack of clothing to wear to school, and the outside employment of school-aged children during school days were realities long before the United States entered the war. From late August 1917 through spring 1918, the national and state press kept the problems of the schools before the reading public. Despite newly enacted laws and prolific rhetoric, however, the war was over before well-intentioned plans could be carried out in full.

The Federal Child Labor Law went into effect on September 1, 1917. Introduced in the U.S. Congress in 1916 as the Keating-Owen Child Labor Act, it was designed to "set free"[297] children under age fourteen who had been working in mills, canneries, and factories, as well as children under sixteen who had been laboring in mines. The law, which President Woodrow Wilson supported, banned articles produced by child labor from being sold through interstate commerce. Its introduction during 1916 confirms two facts: the problem of child labor—and the resulting absence from school—preceded the nation's entry into the war and was not simply a local problem for Arkansas. Although it did not address school attendance—a state responsibility—the federal Child Labor Law and the Arkansas School Attendance Law went hand in hand.[298]

In an article published in newspapers on August 26, 1917, just prior to the child labor law's effective date, Dr. Anna Howard Shaw, chairman of the National Woman's Committee, offered specific steps that women should take in the matter of illiteracy and the betterment of schools. Shaw advised that every woman in the nation should cooperate with the government in making sure that each child of school age attended classes from the very first day of the school year. "So many of our educated young men are in the army and more will follow, and all the more is it incumbent upon us to see that the young people are given the training which will enable them to take up the task of world-rebuilding after the war is over."[299] Shaw urged state divisions of the National Woman's Committee to encourage teachers to become members of the local woman's committee. This was particularly true of rural teachers, "as the teacher is the best person to interest the children and their parents in the lines of service in which the government seeks their co-operation."[300]

In the same article, however, Julia Lathrop viewed the concern in a different light as she reminded women that even full enforcement of the new law would not be enough to ensure a quality education for children released from work. Lathrop reminded women of the nation, "If every child released from work can be sent, well nourished and decently clothed, to a good school, under a good teacher, then the full benefit of the Federal Child Labor law will be reaped for the country's children."[301] Rural children were especially vulnerable because they often lived in areas where the greatest problem of illiteracy existed. Lathrop noted that improved schools would likely require additional taxes. She urged women to work to ensure that all schools were full time, that all teachers were well equipped, and that scholarships were provided in areas of dire poverty.[302]

As the conversation continued through October, the *Arkansas Gazette* printed a synopsis of the eight parts of Arkansas's first compulsory school attendance law:

First	Every child between seven and fifteen years old, both inclusive, must attend some public, private or parochial school at least three-fourths of the session or sessions in the district in which the child resides.
Second	All children must enter school not later than two weeks after the opening of the school term.
Third	The following classes of children between the ages of seven and fifteen, both inclusive, may be excused from attending school for the following reasons: Children mentally or physically incapacitated to perform school duties; Children who have completed the common school course of study, including the seventh grade as outlined by the state superintendent of public instruction; Children whose services are needed to support widowed mother.
Fourth	It is the duty of the attendance officer to investigate all cases of nonattendance and to notify the parents or guardians when the children fail to comply with the provisions of the act.
Fifth	The penalty for nonattendance falls on parent or guardian—maximum fine of ten dollars and costs for each offense.
Sixth	It shall be the duty of the prosecuting attorneys of the state of Arkansas or their deputies to prosecute all violators of this act as in case of any other misdemeanor.
Seventh	It shall be the duty of grand juries to investigate all cases of nonattendance at schools and return indictments in accordance with the evidence and facts.

| Eighth | It shall be the duty of all school boards to provide ample means of publicity, by posting notices or by public announcements, as to the date on which any session of school shall begin—such notice must be given at least 10 days before the beginning of the session of school.[303] |

In the March 1918 issue of its *Educational News Bulletin*, the Arkansas State Department of Education discussed the problems of child labor and school dropouts in the state's farming districts. Although the Federal Child Labor Law dealt with children working in canneries, factories, mills, and mines, Arkansas's children were more likely to miss school to work on their own families' farms. Adults were sometimes overly enthusiastic about growing crops to meet the nation's needs and thus allowed small and half-grown children to miss school for weeks to assist in the work. In these districts, the opening of school had been deferred for a month or more, and the term was cut short in the spring. Even teachers were often in favor of these practices, and at least one county superintendent of schools had instigated the shortening of school days to allow students to work in the fields. The article's author, however, averred that "[t]he biggest thing a boy or girl can do for his country, right now, is to go to school every day. That is his 'bit' and the most effective assistance he can render humanity."[304]

Continuing, the article found that England had made the "dreadful mistake"[305] early on in the war of employing child labor on a wholesale scale. France, on the other hand, had kept its children in school. "Very often they have studied and recited their lessons in deep caves and dug-outs, where the shrieking of shells and roar of cannon could still be heard."[306] After the war, "even though millions of her present generation have passed away,"[307] the coming generation would be as keen of intellect, as well educated, and as ready to rebuild the nation because of France's heroic teachers. And yet, southern cotton mills were asking for eleven- and twelve-year-old children to work eleven hours a day. And other children were forsaking their futures to remain at home to work long days on their fathers' farms.[308]

By the second half of 1918, it was obvious that early provisions, which left absence from school up to the local truancy officer, were not successful. Thus, a "Back-to-the-School Drive" was to be organized by each state's woman's committee in an effort to minimize unlawful child labor and the resulting absence from school. For rural counties, a committee of five members would be organized for each school in the community. Committee members would obtain from the schools' principals names of children who were no longer attending school. Each committee member would be acquainted with school problems, possess necessary tact to make herself welcome in the home, and be sufficiently persistent to get the needed information about the child. After visiting each home, the committee member would turn in a card with information indicating "where there is laxity in the enforcement of our child labor laws and school attendance laws."[309]

A strike among printers, however, delayed the distribution of specific instructions to the states. The transmittal letter, dated November 13, 1918, was optimistic despite the delay, noting that with the end of the war there would be no argument for child labor. Instead, the displacement of temporary laborers by returning soldiers would provide "a clinching argument for a drive to withdraw all children from industry to the protecting and developing influence of the school-house."[310]

Despite the national committee's rather daunting plans, county welfare departments' reports focused on the specific needs of each area. Bradley County reported that—through the sale of Red Cross seals—the department was able to provide a public health nurse for six weeks, during which time she examined every child attending school. The result was "a general awakening on the part of the parents as to minor weaknesses of their children."[311] Many operations on adenoids and tonsils followed her diagnosis. Crawford County reported various activities to increase patriotism among school children as well as endeavors "to develop the idea of using our school buildings for community centers."[312]

In Cross County, the department placed patriotic literature in the schools and urged the sale of liberty bonds and war savings stamps. Johnson County reported that its department had investigated school attendance and urged those not attending to return to school. Members had also pushed the movement for better-educated teachers and more intelligent patriotism and war work. Drew, Mississippi, and Franklin counties reported campaigns that stressed the importance of the back-to-school drive and enforcement of school attendance laws. However, several counties noted that planned back-to-school emphases were disrupted by the Spanish influenza quarantine during the final months of 1918.[313]

Although a true, statewide education system did not develop from 1900 through 1920, Arkansas's schools experienced improvements during the Progressive Era years. A decline in the state's illiteracy rate of individuals ten years of age or older was a measurement of the impact of education. In 1900, 20.4 percent of this group was illiterate; in 1909, the figure was 13.5 percent; and by 1919, this number had dropped to 9.4 percent.[314] One historian noted that school attendance increased from 64 to 71 percent. The average school term increased from 77 to 126 days, and the amount of money spent annually on education per pupil increased from $3.64 to $15.73. Even teacher salaries improved, with the wage of a Grade I male instructor increasing from $38 to $90 monthly.[315]

Despite some apparent improvement during the Progressive Era, author Ben F. Johnson quoted a federal evaluator's early 1920s findings as to Arkansas's schools during the 1910s: "To these children, to be born in Arkansas is a misfortune and an injustice from which they will never recover and upon which they will look back with bitterness when plunged, in adult life, into competition with the children born in other states."[316] Johnson also noted that "with 83 percent of the population living in communities of 2,500 or less and approximately 72 percent on farms, only Mississippi, North and South Dakota were more rural."[317]

Although Arkansas women's wartime attempts to lessen their

community schools' problems were inadequate, once again the intense focus brought on by national leaders simply magnified and led to a frenzied effort to face a social problem that was much larger than each county's women could hope to alleviate.

Chapter 13: Helping Arkansans Survive a Pandemic

"Precautionary measures to prevent the spreading of 'bad colds,' which might prove to be Spanish influenza, have been adopted at Camp Pike, and many individual units have been quarantined as a result of the rapid spread of the disease." [318]

Central Arkansans were gracious hosts for soldiers stationed at the newly constructed Camp Pike as well as for officers in training at Fort Roots [319] in North Little Rock during fall 1917. Toward the end of September, for example, 200 Jewish soldiers from Fort Roots and Camp Pike were entertained with a dinner at the Hotel Marion in Little Rock. The dinner followed a day of fasting in observance of Yom Kippur, the Day of Atonement. Members of the committee on welfare of Jewish soldiers, which included the temple aid Council of Jewish Women, participated in the event. [320] Also in late September, women of the Health and Recreation Association made plans to host, on Saturdays and Sundays, the rest and recreation room planned for enlisted men at the corner of Second and Main streets in Little Rock. The clubroom, which eventually opened in December, was under military supervision and was housed in a loaned second-floor billiards parlor. [321]

By late December, with Christmas Day just three days away, the chairman of the health and recreation department of the Arkansas Woman's Committee announced that she would receive at her Little Rock home women's donations of fruits, flowers, and magazines for the base hospital at Camp Pike. All packages were to be expressed, prepaid, to her home. Department members hoped to receive a red carnation for each hospitalized soldier. Women who were sending fruit in jars were asked to first wrap the jars in paper and place the wrapped jars in the cardboard cartons in which purchased before crating them for mailing. The article continued with assurance that all donations would be delivered to Camp Pike. An update on December 23 noted that—because of bad weather—the shipment of jams and preserves for the base hospital would be delayed. The sweet treats were donated by Daughters of the American Revolution throughout Arkansas.[322]

With the New Year, however, newspaper articles reported various illnesses among soldiers at Camp Pike. On January 18, an article on page three of the *Arkansas Gazette*, titled "Camp Pike Cited for Disease Rate," noted that the camp had recently experienced epidemics of measles, mumps, and scarlet fever; however, much of the illness was brought to the camp with troop transfers from other places. In addition, a virulent form of pneumonia prevailed throughout the nation, both in civilian and military life. Six days later, on January 24, the *Gazette* reported thirty deaths from pneumonia at the camp during the preceding week. On July 19, Camp Pike announced that its population had soared to 50,000 men; three canvas camps had been erected to shelter the new arrivals. Then, on September 19, an article titled "Influenza Spreads in New England" noted that the disease had also appeared at New Orleans and Camp Jackson, South Carolina.[323]

Despite knowledge of past epidemics at the camp from as far back as January, as well as an overflowing population of 50,000 recruits just north of Little Rock, Arkansans seemed oblivious to the possibility of a pandemic that was about to engulf their towns and countryside. But on September 26, 1918, the *Arkansas Gazette* reported that "precautionary measures to prevent the spreading of 'bad colds,' which might prove to be Spanish influenza, have been adopted at Camp Pike, and many individual units have been quarantined as a result of the rapid spread of the disease."[324] Ten days later, on October 6, the *Gazette* reported that 13,000 cases of Spanish influenza had been identified at the cantonment.[325]

As the epidemic spread to the civilian population and paralyzed the entire state, Dr. James C. Geiger, U.S. Public Health Officer for Arkansas, contacted the state Woman's Committee, which referred his request to its home economics department for help in providing nourishment to families unable to take care of themselves.[326] In Little

Rock, the county home demonstration agent, assisted by five field agents who were not able to do their work because of the quarantine, organized a so-called "diet kitchen" and got it up and running in a few days.[327] Later, the entire responsibility of providing supplies and delivering food to the homes of the sick in central Arkansas was taken over by Little Rock women through efforts of the Council of Defense for Arkansas and other organizations. Over 2,000 people were provided soup and other sustenance.[328]

Most of the state's sixty-eight home demonstration kitchens were converted into diet kitchens, and at least thirty county agents provided similar services in smaller towns and rural communities, in cooperation with the home economics department of each county council of defense. Miller County reported that during the influenza epidemic, members of the woman's committee, through the church societies, "did splendid work in making and delivering soup free from the government kitchen to the sick." Montgomery County reported helping many during the influenza epidemic.[329]

Reports from other counties offer additional tidbits, confirming women's contributions. On October 5, Dr. G. D. Huddleston called the Faulkner County Council of Defense, asking for volunteer practical nurses to be used in an influenza epidemic at the SATC barracks[330] and Hendrix College in Conway. Immediately, the woman's committee went over the registration cards and secured names of 158 women who had registered to help in such an emergency. "The women of Conway responded nobly, and out of about 400 cases we only lost two of the boys."[331] Montgomery County gave "all possible assistance"[332] during the influenza epidemic.

In Washington County, the woman's committee organized and coordinated nurses to tend to ill students at the University of Arkansas. Craighead and Clark counties also reported significant support from women who had registered for service as practical nurses. Hempstead County reported that rural women were given every assistance during the epidemic, and "nursing and caring for children when they were ill was the special work of the committee."[333]

In Pulaski County, the Council of Jewish Women assisted in notifying by telephone 200 women who had registered to be trained as practical nurses, "endeavoring to get them to volunteer their services during the influenza epidemic. This necessitated making constant telephone calls from 9:00 a.m. to 5:00 p.m., and over 30 women responded."[334] And the Polk County report, which provided insights used throughout this study, noted that a woman with an office downtown "helped to place nurses, had typewritten forms for treatment and how to prevent contagion, and in one day distributed one hundred of these leaflets to the rural communities."[335]

The influenza epidemic was unimaginably devastating. It killed more people in one year than the Black Death did in an entire century. In Arkansas, about 7,000 people died from the disease. Many rural deaths went unreported. Sometimes families were wiped out because no one had the strength to draw water or prepare food. Although rural people were known for helping each other, they generally could not or would not help their neighbors.[336] Once again—although without instructions from Washington—home demonstration agents and the organization of women throughout the state under the umbrella of the Arkansas Woman's Committee were a godsend to the people of Arkansas.

Chapter 14: Experiencing Political Change

"Although there were disappointments for women, the overall session was considered a splendid session of splendid deeds and will go down in history as one that had a vision of the human needs of the state."[337]

During the war, Arkansas women's efforts toward voting rights gained significant momentum; however, the journey's first recorded step was neither encouraging nor enduring. As Arkansas's representatives gathered for the state's constitutional convention of 1868, Miles Ledford Langley of Clark County surprised his colleagues by proposing the enfranchisement of women. After the proposal was "ridiculed into silence,"[338] the issue lay dormant in the political arena until the 1880s.[339] The majority of women—as well as men—were apathetic toward suffrage. Even the Arkansas Federation of Women's Clubs did not embrace the movement until 1915—the eleventh hour.[340] Clerics preached sermons against the movement, and anti-suffragists claimed that women would not vote if they could; on the other hand, those who wanted the vote would neglect home and family for politics. By the 1880s, however, women who favored suffrage began to meet and advocate for it.[341]

In the decades preceding the war, Arkansas's women were already lobbying for governmental reform through the statewide network of women's organizations under the umbrella of the AFWC. Issues included women's property rights and creation of a reform school for women. Concern for children was also high on their agenda. Women advocated for a child welfare department, child labor laws, state industrial schools for boys and girls, and the use of schools as social centers. As women "began to view government as the agency to produce the reforms they wanted,"[342] many advocated for their participation in the election of public officials. Although all members of women's clubs did not advocate for suffrage, those who did usually came from within the organizations.[343]

Despite its initial opposition to suffrage, the *Woman's Chronicle*, published in Little Rock in the 1880s by Catherine Campbell Cuningham, took an about-face as it embraced the idea of women's suffrage. In answer to anti-suffragists' questioning as to whether women wanted suffrage, its December 6, 1888, issue opined, "Our experience is that whenever an unprejudiced, uninfluenced woman takes the matter under consideration, she sees at once its justice, and becomes one of its supporters."[344] Finding that the power of the ballot was surely responsible for men's higher wages for identical work, the article noted that within three years, the number of suffragists in the South had increased from almost nil to "legion."[345]

Also during 1888, Clara A. McDiarmid gathered thirteen like-minded friends and organized the first Little Rock Suffrage Association. Five years later, McDiarmid was elected president of the Arkansas Equal Suffrage Association, which had members in Beebe, Forrest City, Fort Smith, Hazen, Hope, Hot Springs, Malvern, Morrilton, Ozark, Rogers, and Stuttgart. However, McDiarmid's death in 1899 "stilled the suffrage movement in Arkansas for a number of years."[346]

Although the campaign for women's suffrage was long-suffering, in 1911, the newly formed Political Equality League (PEL) at Little Rock, made up primarily of middle-class women, was able to create a legislative discussion of suffrage; no legislation resulted from the increased awareness. However, by 1914, the suffrage movement had expanded throughout the state, with branches of the PEL in several towns and cities. At a state meeting that year, the Arkansas Woman Suffrage Association was organized.[347] With the United States' entry into the war, suffrage efforts did not cease.

During 1917 and 1918, even as Arkansas's sons and brothers fought in violent battles in Europe, its daily newspapers dispersed news of suffrage and other enfranchisement efforts on two fronts: the national stage, exemplified in Washington DC, and the Arkansas stage, which dealt with state and local primary elections. Few newspaper articles mentioned Arkansas women rallying for national suffrage. Instead, according to newspaper coverage, the state's women were concerned with the questions of paying poll taxes and voting in local primaries.

Little Rock, January 1917: As the Arkansas state legislature met for its regular session in January 1917, it seemed that only a constitutional convention could provide a pathway to suffrage in state elections for Arkansas's women. Although Representative John A. Riggs of Garland County had initially proposed a constitutional amendment early in the regular session, he withdrew the measure because it was too late for its submission at the next general election. In his inaugural message before the state legislature soon afterward, Governor Charles Brough made clear his support of women's suffrage in Arkansas. Having stated that Arkansas's women should have a voice in "all questions affecting property, education and morality of the commonwealth and our beloved state,"[348] Brough vowed to use whatever personal and political influence he might have to ensure the incorporation of such a provision in a new state constitution.[349]

Little Rock, March 1917: The Forty-first General Assembly of the State of Arkansas passed into history. Women counted their gains, which they considered to be numerous. Amid almost one thousand bills introduced during the two-month session, several that became law during the final week were considered to be of benefit to women: the Riggs primary suffrage bill; bills providing for a board of charities and correction and for mothers' pensions; appropriations for the boys' and girls' industrial school (although considered much too small); appropriations for state aid to high schools; a bill to regulate commerce in the products of child labor; and a bill providing for a juvenile court in both county sites when a county had two separate sites. Although there were disappointments for women, the overall session was considered "a splendid session of splendid deeds and will go down in history as one that had a vision of the human needs of the state."[350]

Newspaper contributor Minnie U. Rutherford-Fuller continued by encouraging newly enfranchised women to go to the polls on primary election days. Although all men were not held accountable if some men failed to vote from year to year, she argued that women had to vote at each opportunity so that women as a whole would not be disenfranchised. Noting that "the average woman in this state is perhaps better educated than the average man,"[351] Rutherford-Fuller found that women had no excuse for not voting intelligently. "More of our girls than boys have been going through our high schools for a generation and fewer of them have been truant in attendance upon schools of all kinds; for various reasons, or no reason at all, our girls have had better moral training also and for every advantage there is a corresponding obligation."[352] Rutherford-Fuller also encouraged club women to make the study of candidates and office-holding a priority.[353]

Within less than a week of the passage of the Riggs legislation, Sebastian County officials sought a legal opinion after nine women paid their fee in order to register to vote. By March 18, Attorney General John D. Arbuckle ruled that women should be permitted to pay their poll tax, which was not required under the Riggs act. However, because the act did not go into effect until June 30, they would not be allowed to vote in the April primaries for nomination of delegates to the constitutional convention. Later, women were notified that June 25 would be the last day on which they could assess and pay their poll tax in order to vote in the first primary held after the June 30 effective date. By the end of 1917, Sebastian County would again play a role as the site of the first primary in which women would vote.[354]

Washington DC, Summer 1917: Members of the national Woman's Party managed to make daily newspapers as they picketed the White House in pursuit of women's suffrage, held song services for fellow prisoners after being escorted to jail, accepted pardons from President Woodrow Wilson, and then continued to heckle him after their release. However, on July 22, the AFWC page of the *Arkansas Gazette* carried an open letter to the public from the National American Woman Suffrage Association, which purportedly represented 98 percent of the organized suffragists of the United States. In the letter, the association went on record as disapproving the picketing tactics of the Woman's Party.[355]

Washington DC, September 1917: The U.S. House of Representatives voted 181 to 107 to create a standing committee on women's suffrage. The Ways and Means Committee would name members of the new committee, which would assume charge of all suffrage bills previously handled by the "strongly anti-suffrage Judiciary Committee."[356] Creation of the newly authorized committee would ensure an early fight on the Susan B. Anthony suffrage amendment at the next session of Congress. All members of the Arkansas delegation voted for creation of the standing committee. In the meantime, once again, four White House picketers were arrested but released on bond to appear the next day.[357]

New York, October 1917: In a speech before one hundred members of the New York state women's suffrage party, President Wilson noted that the time was right for men of all parties to vote for women's suffrage. Wilson commented that "[t]he whole world now is witnessing a struggle between two ideals of government. It is a struggle which goes deeper and touches more of the foundations of the organized life of men than any struggle that has ever taken place before."[358] He also noted that he considered this a time for the states of the Union to take action in favor of equal suffrage. Having found that the country depended on women for much of its inspiration, under war conditions the country also depended on women for service, which they had "rendered in abundance and with the distinction of originality."[359]

Fort Smith, November 1917: The first test of women's right to vote in a local Arkansas primary election took place in Fort Smith. Headlines predicted the heaviest vote in the city's history as both men and women came out to cast their votes for mayor. Four hundred twenty-two women had paid their poll tax and were eligible to vote. The two candidates were Arch Monroe and J. H. Wright; Wright had recently been deposed as mayor, following his conviction for making a pre-election campaign promise. The Wednesday, November

14, headline gave the news: "Wright Defeated by Women's Vote."[360] Monroe had defeated Wright by 192 votes. Although Wright filed suit, asking for a recount, the local circuit judge refused to sign an injunction to prevent the subsequent election.[361]

Little Rock, November and December 1917: During late 1917 and throughout 1918, Arkansas's women were neither isolated from news of other women's efforts nor were they laboring in a vacuum. Arkansas was frequently a stopover for well-known activists of the time, and daily newspapers provided stories of women's efforts throughout the nation. In early November 1917, Arkansas's suffragists gave a frosty reception to Jane Pincus, a representative of the national Woman's Party, whose members had picketed the White House. Pincus visited Little Rock in hopes of organizing a branch of the Woman's Party. Two weeks later, Jeanette Rankin of Montana, the first woman elected to the U.S. House of Representatives, was warmly welcomed to Little Rock by a delegation of suffrage leaders and representatives of the Little Rock woman teachers' association. Rankin lectured on "democracy in government" at the high school auditorium that evening.[362]

Little Rock, December 1917: Florence B. Cotnam, nationally known suffragist and recently elected chairman of Arkansas's Equal Suffrage Central Committee, wrote an open letter to Arkansas's suffragists, calling 1918 a time of great opportunity for the activists. Noting that passage of both national and state constitutional amendments would require sacrifices of time, labor, and money, Cotnam averred that the time was ripe because "our country never needed us as it does now."[363] Cotnam also noted that both Republicans and Democrats would likely vote for women's suffrage since history had shown that newly enfranchised populations tended to vote for the party that had enfranchised them.[364]

Washington DC, January 1918: On the national level, each of Arkansas's seven members of the U.S. House of Representatives voted for a January 7, 1918, resolution to submit the national suffrage amendment to states for ratification. With dramatic flair, the resolution carried by only one vote. Two representatives reportedly left their sick beds to vote for the measure, which passed with a vote of 274 to 136. A test vote in the U.S. Senate in May had a different outcome. The vote was forty to twenty-one, one less than the necessary two-thirds vote.[365]

Throughout Arkansas, February 1918: During the statewide registration-for-service campaign, women in rural areas in Arkansas's counties voiced opposition to the suffrage movement as they refused to register for service. One county reported that "[a] prominent war worker who ought to have known better said she would not register because it was the work of the suffragists, and was not authorized by the president."[366] Another reported that women did not want "to become converts to woman suffrage."[367] In another county, women refused to register due to "[f]ear of being forced to vote."[368]

Little Rock, April 1918: The state's suffrage advocates' attention was focused on the primary elections and constitutional convention as the Arkansas Equal Suffrage Committee planned its statewide annual conference in the Hotel Marion ballroom, beginning on April 2, 1918. Although patriotism would be the key note of the meeting, the organization's agenda was overflowing with pressing issues: winning the war; having full suffrage written into the body of the new state constitution; urging all women to pay the poll tax; and ensuring that women voted in the all-important primary election on May 28. In the upcoming election, a U.S. senator, congressman, and governor would be nominated, as well as all state, county, and district officials. Advocates urged that women had to make every effort to vote since "those officeholders who are responsible for the progress and for the maintenance of a high moral standard in Arkansas will be chosen at that time."[369] And one other reason was given for women to vote in the May primaries:

Arkansas is one of the few states where the alien enemy may vote; that is a foreigner who has signified his intention to become a citizen, and has his first papers, may have a voice in electing the officials of the state. The Kaiser will have an undue influence in the government of Arkansas unless the loyal American women vote in large numbers. There are three times as many foreign-born men as women in the United States. I believe this proportion will hold good in Arkansas.

Patriotism demands that the women of Arkansas cast good American votes for American principles.—Florence B. Cotnam, Chairman[370]

Cotnam correctly described a state law allowing immigrants to vote in state elections after they had filed papers indicating their intention to become citizens. During the war—as anti-German sentiment was strong throughout Arkansas—the concern was that German immigrants would be allowed to vote. On April 18, the Committee on Suffrage and Elections of Arkansas's constitutional convention proposed elimination of the provision.[371]

Little Rock, April 1918: Committees of Arkansas's constitutional convention had begun their work. The committees' decisions were neither binding nor final but provided a working basis for the convention. The joint Committee on Suffrage and Elections was the first to complete its task. Using the present constitution as a basis, the committee declared unanimously for equal suffrage and quadrennial elections; elimination of the provision for non-citizens to vote, based on their declared intentions to become citizens; and prohibition of laws requiring the registration of electors.[372]

Atlanta, Georgia, and Hot Springs, Arkansas, May 1918: Word of two major Protestant groups' activities toward women's equality made its way to Arkansas. From Atlanta came word that the general conference of the Methodist Episcopal Church, South (a precursor of the United Methodist Church) had heard the reading of papers asking that women of the church be given every right of the church, not only as members but as church officials. Twelve days later, news from the national conference of the Southern Baptist Convention, meeting in Hot Springs, noted that women of the church were granted full and equal rights with men within the convention. Women's newly granted rights thus included representing their churches at annual conferences and holding any office in the convention.[373]

Washington DC, June 1918: President Wilson once again offered his influence into the battle:

> The services of women during this supreme crisis of the world's history have been of the most signal usefulness and distinction. The war could not have been fought without them, or its sacrifices endured. It is high time that some part of our debt of gratitude to them should be acknowledged and paid, and the only acknowledgement they ask is their admission to the suffrage. Can we justly refuse it? As for America, it is my earnest hope that the Senate of the United States will give an unmistakable answer to this question by passing the suffrage amendment to our federal constitution before the end of this session.[374]

As in his October 1917 endorsement of women's suffrage, President Wilson had alluded to women's contributions to the war effort as the compelling reason to pass the suffrage amendment to the U.S. Constitution. A comparison of the two speeches, however, reveals a more convincing endorsement following eight additional months of war.

Little Rock, July 1918: Members of Arkansas's constitutional convention met on the first Monday in July, and with only one dissenting vote, delegates endorsed full suffrage for women. Because some delegates did not approve of women serving on juries (purportedly because of ungentlemanly conduct in some jury rooms), the convention agreed to make such service optional. However, an attempt to prohibit women from holding public office was soundly defeated by a vote of sixty-three to three. Delegates also endorsed the national women's suffrage amendment, asked the U.S. Senate to pass it, and, in the event of its adoption, asked the House and Senate of 1919 to ratify it.[375]

Texas and Arkansas, September 1918: Women's political prospects nationally and state wide seemed to be improving. In Texas, a woman was named chairman of the State Democratic Convention, and the national Republican Party organized the Republican Women's National Executive Committee. In Arkansas, the proposed constitution was printed in local newspapers. Article III, Suffrage, Franchise and Elections, section one, stated: "The right to vote or to hold office shall not be denied or abridged on account of sex. Male and female citizens shall enjoy equally all civil, political and religious rights and privileges, but women shall not be compelled to serve as jurors."[376]

Washington DC, September 1918: However, in the U.S. Senate, prospects were not encouraging. On September 27, after a day of bitter debate in which senators' confidential negotiations were publicly disclosed, the Senate adjourned until the next day. Although suffrage advocates were hoping for a vote, opponents threatened a filibuster to prevent a roll call until the following Monday since many senators would be absent on Saturday, making Liberty Loan speeches. On Wednesday, October 2, the disheartening news reached Arkansas's newspapers: "Woman Suffrage Beaten in Senate."[377] The vote was fifty-four for to thirty against, two short of the needed two-thirds majority.

Arkansas, December 1918: The new Arkansas constitution was submitted for ratification in December 1918. The *Arkansas Gazette* published an editorial that read: "Vote to enfranchise Arkansas women, not only as a reward for their services and sacrifices in war, but for the good of the state."[378] Despite Arkansas women's relentless campaign, the proposed constitution failed by some 13,000 votes. In addition to suffrage, Progressive Era women's concerns dealing with prohibition of alcohol, children's health and well-being, and education were included in the proposed document. The defeat was blamed on bad weather, lingering effects of the influenza epidemic, and light voter turnout. However, unpopular provisions within the constitution, including taxation, prohibition, and the initiative and referendum, also contributed.[379]

When the state legislature met in January 1919, sentiment was running high for women's suffrage. Both houses of the state legislature approved two measures within a few days: (1) a suffrage amendment to the Arkansas constitution; and, (2) a resolution that asked Congress to submit for ratification by the states a federal suffrage amendment to the U.S. Constitution. The first measure was approved, with an amendment not to compel women to serve as jurors; it would be placed on the statewide ballot in the next general election. Because of a technicality, which was later overturned by the Arkansas Supreme Court, the amendment to Arkansas's constitution did not pass. However, in 1926, following the overturning of the technicality, the Arkansas attorney general issued an opinion that the equal suffrage amendment to the Arkansas constitution was then in force.[380]

In the meantime, the U.S. Congress approved the federal women's suffrage amendment during June 1919 and submitted it to the states for ratification. Wasting no time, Governor Brough set July 28 for a special session of the legislature. The Senate approved the amendment by a vote of twenty-nine to two; the House approved it by seventy-four to fifteen. Arkansas thus became the second state in the South and the twelfth state in the nation to ratify the Nineteenth Amendment to the U.S. Constitution.[381]

Conclusion

Arkansas's women had come through for "the boys" in the trenches in Europe; for the allies, who had suffered unfathomable losses during more than four years of war; and for the nation. They had put forth great effort to fulfill every request that was made of them. Women who were already organized accepted leadership roles on the Arkansas Woman's Committee. In their newly created positions, they successfully spurred other women—even those in rural areas who often were not adequately informed—to join in the cause. Home demonstration agents of the Cooperative Extension Service, who were joined by home economics teachers, provided invaluable technical advice to homemakers attempting to place appealing meals on the family dinner table despite shortages of essential commodities. And women of all economic classes accepted their roles as stewards of the scarce foods available to them.

Arkansas women's first major wartime responsibility was in the kitchen. Some attempted to raise gardens and to can the produce despite their fears that the government might come into their homes and confiscate the family's winter food supply. As wheat became scarce, they managed to bake bread with substitutes for half the wheat. As meat became scarce, they made one meal into two or three by serving stews and soups. Home demonstration agents encouraged women to make meat dishes by pan-frying cottage cheese coated with cornmeal and to concoct desserts by stuffing prunes with peanuts. Because the previous several years had been prosperous, however, women sometimes balked at the prospect of doing without. Their leaders then admonished them with reminders that skimping on food was their patriotic duty and that the army that was able to hold out the longest would win the war.

Within a few weeks of the nation's entry into the war, Arkansas's women reported to Red Cross workrooms to construct hospital supplies for military medical units in Europe. The American Red Cross created a finely oiled machine as its leaders provided instructions and instructors for its myriad workrooms, many in rural areas of Arkansas. Bandage rolling had been honed to a fine art form as national leaders consulted doctors in Europe to determine the exact bandages most needed in the field. And local instructors had to be able to supervise eager, willing workers, many of whom had no applicable skills. As workrooms received orders to lay aside their inventories of hospital supplies, volunteers immediately picked up their needles and began knitting winter clothing. Women who could not leave their homes followed instructions printed in local newspapers. By December 1917, workrooms had extended daily hours to incorporate evening shifts in order to meet increased demands for bandages.

Job vacancies created by wartime conditions provided the seeming possibility of women's entry into higher-paying positions previously filled by men. However, the tendency of single women to treat jobs as temporary stopgaps until marriage fostered men's resentment over their willingness to take "men's jobs," but for less pay. At the same time, the Arkansas Woman's Committee strove to ensure that employers observed minimum wage and maximum hour laws for women. As women in other regions of the country garnered higher wages in unionized factory positions, some of Arkansas's female employees went on strike for better wages and working conditions. As a result of conflicting reactions to wartime opportunities, the state's young single women endured experiences in the workplace that foreshadowed a long road to more equitable treatment. On the other hand, shortages in two professions led to campaigns for additional women to take up the work. Young high school graduates were urged to become teachers, even though women already occupied the majority of positions throughout the state. In the relatively new nursing profession, which was already exclusively filled by women, dire shortages resulted in greater respect as incumbents' contributions proved to be invaluable.

On December 11, 1918, the war ended. Women had contributed significantly to the wartime effort. They had responded valiantly to every request sent down from the National Woman's Committee and the American Red Cross Woman's Bureau. They had worked for improved children's health, better schools, fewer child laborers, and a safer environment in the state's large cantonment city. When the Spanish influenza epidemic struck Arkansas in late September 1918, women organized to feed and to provide support to thousands of families—as well as college students away from home—who were suffering from the devastating illness. In all of these endeavors, Arkansas women's contributions were predominately a reflection of who they were. Their place was in the home, and they were still providers of moral strength to the family. As temperance advocate Carry Nation had declared, although a woman's place may be in the home, home is wherever our loved ones are, and "a woman would be either selfish or cowardly"[382] if she refused to leave her home to relieve suffering or trouble.[383]

The role of Arkansas's women showed little evidence of gradually changing during the twenty-three years between the end of one world war and the beginning of the next. A devastating twenty-year economic depression that affected most Arkansans had seen to that. Many families were focused on survival. In an essay titled "Diluting an Institution: The Social Impact of World War II on the Arkansas Family," historian C. Calvin Smith confirmed that the state's women and their families had not changed dramatically by the beginning of World War II. Smith noted:

> The Victorian idea of a strong, providing father supported by a faithful wife-mother who took care of the home and properly trained and disciplined children was alive and well in Arkansas when the United States entered World War II in December 1941. And there was a strong demand to continue the tradition despite the demands made upon the state's women by a nation at war.[384]

With the continuing Victorian tradition of mothers as protectors and moral agents for their families, the Great War did not create lasting changes for Arkansas's women. But the next war did. The title of

139

Smith's essay, which alludes to the erosion of the traditional Arkansas family during World War II, hints at the changes to come in the following seventy-five years and beyond. The women of Arkansas prepared to take the first steps of that journey with their efforts both at home and in the workplace during World War I.

Notes

1   Report of the Woman's Committee, Council of Defense for Arkansas (hereafter, Report of the Arkansas Woman's Committee), "Reports of County Councils," Arkansas State Archives, Little Rock (ASA/LR). In her final report, the Greene County Woman's Committee chairman noted, "We feel that we deserve a creditable record in Arkansas history, for we have been faithful to our tasks."

2   "Donate Site for School," *Arkansas Gazette*, January 31, 1917.

3   Page Smith, *America Enters the World: A People's History of the Progressive Era and World War I*, vol. 7 (New York: McGraw-Hill, 1985), 567.

4   The name of the organization was referred to in various configurations, particularly during its first few weeks. For consistency, Woman's Committee, Council of Defense for Arkansas ("Arkansas Woman's Committee") will be used throughout.

5   Report of the Arkansas Woman's Committee, 68, ASA/LR.

6   "Withdraws Equal Suffrage Measure," *Arkansas Gazette*, January 24, 1917.

7   "Legislature Has Gone into History," *Arkansas Gazette*, March 11, 1917.

8   For an excellent discussion of Arkansas's club women, see Frances Mitchell Ross, "The New Woman as Club Woman and Social Activist in Turn of the Century Arkansas," *Arkansas Historical Quarterly* 50 (Winter 1991): 317–51.

9   Ibid.

10   Report of the Arkansas Woman's Committee, "Reports of County Councils," ASA/LR.

11   "Defines Relation of Two Governmental Organizations," *Arkansas Gazette*, August 12, 1917.

12   Despite various configurations of its name, the term "Council of National Defense" will be used throughout the remainder of this book.

13   Report of the Arkansas State Council of Defense ("Council of Defense for Arkansas"), May 22, 1917, to July 1, 1919. Council of Defense Records, 4; on file at the Arkansas State Archives, Little Rock, Arkansas (ASA/LR). The report quoted two separate clauses from the Army Appropriation Act, which have been placed within the quotation above. Despite various configurations of its name, the term "Council of Defense for Arkansas" will be used throughout.

14   Ibid.

15 Ibid., 4–5.

16 Despite various configurations of its name, the term "Woman's Com-mittee, Council of National Defense" ("National Woman's Committee") will be used throughout.

17 "Defines Relation of Two Governmental Organizations," *Arkansas Gazette*, August 12, 1917.

18 Ibid.

19 "Women Organize to Conserve Food," *Arkansas Gazette*, July 3, 1917.

20 "Arkansas Women Called Into Service by State Division," *Arkansas Gazette*, July 15, 1917.

21 The letter, dated June 22, was apparently sent by telegram.

22 Letter, Woman's Committee, Council of National Defense, to chair-men, state councils of defense, June 22, 1917, file 234, Council of De-fense Records, ASA/LR.

23 Ibid.

24 Ibid.

25 "Call for Heads of Women's Societies," *Arkansas Gazette*, June 24, 1917; "Women Organize to Save Food," *Arkansas Gazette*, July 8, 1917.

26 "Arkansas Women Called Into Service by State Division," *Arkansas Gazette*, July 15, 1917.

27 Ibid.

28 Report of the Arkansas Woman's Committee, 15, ASA/LR.

29 Letter, Ida Frauenthal to Wallace Townsend, Chairman, State Council of National Defense, August 16, 1917, folder 234, Council of Defense Records, ASA/LR.

30 "Women Helping the Fighter to Fight," *Arkansas Gazette*, August 5, 1917.

31 "Negro Women Signing," *Arkansas Gazette*, September 9, 1917.

32 "65 Chairmen Working," *Arkansas Gazette*, September 19, 1917.

33 Ibid.

34 "3,582 Sign Pledge to Conserve Food," *Arkansas Gazette*, Septem-ber 12, 1917.

35 "Food Congress Ends," *Arkansas Gazette*, September 28, 1917.

36 "Week of Campaign for Conservation," *Arkansas Gazette*, October 6, 1917.

37 Ibid.

38 "Pledge Cards Have Been Distributed," *Arkansas Gazette*, October 25, 1917.

39 Ibid.

40 "Already Many Pledge Cards Are Being Sent the Administrator," *Arkansas Gazette*, October 26, 1917.

41 "Food Campaign Will Open Today," *Arkansas Gazette*, October 28, 1917.

42 Ibid.

43 "Economy Not a Fad, but a Necessity," *Arkansas Gazette*, October 28, 1917.

44 Ibid.

45 Likely Mrs. C. E. Whitney, publicity chairman of the Arkansas Woman's Committee.

46 "Economy Not a Fad, but a Necessity," *Arkansas Gazette*, October 28, 1917.

47 Ibid.

48 Ibid.

49 "Enemy Agents Into Pledge Campaign," *Arkansas Gazette*, November 1, 1917; "Organization Gives Them Opportunity," *Arkansas Gazette*, October 30, 1917; "Women's Council of Defense Work," *Arkansas Gazette*, November 7, 1917; "Pledge Cards May Still Be Sent In," *Arkansas Gazette*, November 9, 1917.

50 "Directions How to Conserve Food," *Arkansas Gazette*, July 8, 1917.

51 Report of the Arkansas Woman's Committee, 15, ASA/LR.

52 Report of the Arkansas Woman's Committee, "Reports of County Councils," ASA/LR.

53 "Food Prices Up 19 Per Cent in Year," *Arkansas Gazette*, March 13, 1917; "Sugar 50 Cents Pound," *Arkansas Gazette*, June 17, 1917.

54 "The Home Garden—an Essay by Union Trust Company," *Arkansas Gazette*, March 5, 1917.

55 Ibid.

56 "Women in 1,200,000 Homes to Do Nation a Service by Eliminating Garbage Pail," *Arkansas Gazette*, June 20, 1917.

57 Ibid.

58 Advertisement placed by Little Rock Master Bakers, *Arkansas Gazette*, July 12, 1917.

59 "'Tote Your Own Bundles' is New War Slogan," *Arkansas Gazette*, July 1, 1917.

60 Ibid.

61 "Cutting Down Deliveries to Release Men for War," *Arkansas Gazette*, August 5, 1917.

62 "To Carry Own Parcels," *Arkansas Gazette*, August 19, 1917.

63 Advertisement placed by Stifft's Jewelers, *Arkansas Gazette*, December 2, 1917; advertisement placed by M. M. Cohn Company, *Arkansas Gazette*, July 14, 1918.

64 Elizabeth Griffin Hill, *A Splendid Piece of Work 1912–2012: One Hundred Years of Arkansas's Home Demonstration and Extension Homemakers Clubs* (n.p.: 2012),14.

65 Although the Arkansas Woman's Committee's final report covered the period July 1, 1917, through December 30, 1918, the statistics in Bonslagel's report may have been for 1918 only.

66 The home demonstration work in Arkansas was segregated through 1965. African American agents were employed in counties in which the population of black women was sufficient to merit a separate agent.

67 Report of the Arkansas Woman's Committee, ASA/LR; 1918 Annual Narrative Report for Northwest District Home Demonstration Agent, Record Group 33 (RG 33), Arkansas Cooperative Extension Service, National Archives and Records Administration (NARA), Fort Worth, Texas.

68 *Arkansas Gazette*, November 4, 1917.

69 "Federal Control of Sugar is Next," *Arkansas Gazette*, September 12, 1917.

70 "Culling Poultry Flocks Necessary," *Arkansas Gazette*, November 25, 1917; "Use More Poultry; Save Other Meat," *Arkansas Gazette*, January 27, 1918.

71 "Names Meatless, Wheatless Days," *Arkansas Gazette*, November 6, 1917; "Use More Poultry; Save Other Meat," *Arkansas Gazette*, January 27, 1918.

72 "New Conservation Schedule is Out," *Arkansas Gazette*, January 17, 1918.

73 "War Menus, Meatless Meals, Wheat Flour Substitutes," *Arkansas Gazette*, December 9, 1917.

74 Ibid.

75 "Substitutes for Wheat, Their Use," *Arkansas Gazette*, March 31, 1918.

76 1919 Annual Narrative Report, Arkansas Cooperative Extension Service, RG 33, NARA, Fort Worth, Texas.

77 "Camouflaging the Cottage Cheese," *Arkansas Gazette*, May 16, 1918.

78 Circular 109, *Cottage Cheese Dishes* (U.S. Government Printing Office, 1918).

79 "Substitutes for Wheat, Their Use," *Arkansas Gazette*, March 31, 1918.

80 "Are Denied Sugar for the Rest of Year," *Arkansas Gazette*, June 16, 1918; "Certificates for Buyers of Sugar," *Arkansas Gazette*, January 26, 1918.

81 "Certificates for Buyers of Sugar," *Arkansas Gazette*, July 28, 1918; "A Demonstration of the Preservation of Fruit Juices and Jams Without the Use of Sugar," *Arkansas Gazette*, July 14, 1918; "To Increase the Yield of Jelly," *Arkansas Gazette*, August 11, 1918; "Eat the Prunes and Save the Pits," *Arkansas Gazette*, August 29, 1918: "Free the pit of the pulp and dry thoroughly either by means of the sun or the oven. Place the pits in the containers provided for them in the downtown stores, etc. Two hundred pits or seven pounds of nut shells will make enough carbon for one gas mask, which may save the life of a soldier."

82 "To Make Candy Without Sugar," *Arkansas Gazette*, September 22, 1918. (Just as restaurateurs were not required to limit patrons' choices, candy store owners were allowed to place full-sugar treats in front windows and the most visible places in the establishment.)

83 "How Corn Sugar May be Utilized," *Arkansas Gazette*, October 6, 1918.

84 By this time, the "Arkansas Federation of Women's Clubs" page of the *Arkansas Gazette* had been renamed "The Woman's Page."

85 "Cranberries and Sugar Saving," *Arkansas Gazette*, October 13, 1918.

86 Ibid.

87 "How Corn Sugar May be Utilized," *Arkansas Gazette*, October 6, 1918.

88 Ibid.

89 Report of the Arkansas Woman's Committee, "Reports of County Councils." ASA/LR.

90 Ibid.

91 Ibid.

92 "Economy Not a Fad, but a Necessity," *Arkansas Gazette*, October 28, 1917.

93 Thomas J. Schlereth, *Victorian America: Transformations in Everyday Life 1876–1915* (New York: HarperPerennial, 1992), 141.

94 Ibid.

95 Ibid., 142.

96 Ibid.

97 Ibid.

98 Ibid., 141.

99 Whey is the watery liquid that separates from the solid part of milk when it turns sour or when enzymes are added in cheese making.

100 Anna B. Hamman, "The Fireless Cooker," *American Journal of Nursing* 10, no. 9 (June 1910): 652: "The purchased fireless cooker consisted of a box containing one, two, or more compartments for kettles. The kettles fit closely in the compartments and had tight-fitting covers. The space between the compartments and the outside box was filled, usually, with mineral wool, an excellent non-conductor of heat. Homemade cookers resembled the shop-made cookers, and with both the material to be cooked was heated thoroughly in the ordinary way over the fire, then covered closely and put into a tight box packed with some non-conducting material, such as hay or excelsior, through which the heat passed very slowly. While the heat was retained, it did the cooking."

101 A Google search revealed no definition or description of drirambo.

102 "Woman 88 Years Old Works for Red Cross," *Arkansas Gazette*, September 23, 1917.

103 Ida Clyde Clarke, *American Women and the World War* (New York: D. Appleton and Company, 1918), 138.

104 Ibid., 137.

105 Ibid.

106 Minutes, Thirtieth Annual Meeting of the WMU, April 10–12, 1918, Arkansas Baptist State Convention Collection, Riley-Hickingbotham Library Archives and Special Collections, Ouachita Baptist University, Arkadelphia, AR; Report of the Arkansas Woman's Committee, 68.

107 Arkansas Society of the Daughters of the American Revolution, MSS 97-21, Box 1, File 2, Butler Center for Arkansas Studies, Central Arkansas Library System, Little Rock, Arkansas (hereafter, BC/CALS); National Society of Colonial Dames of America, 1899–1999. UALR. MS.0054, Box 3, file 1, Record Book, Vol. II, 1912–1925, University of

Arkansas at Little Rock Center for Arkansas History and Culture (hereafter, CAHC).

108 Report of the Arkansas Woman's Committee, 68, ASA/LR.

109 "Make 700 Articles for Army Hospital," *Arkansas Gazette*, June 17, 1917.

110 Clarke, 140.

111 Ibid., 141.

112 Ibid., 139.

113 Although Clarke mentioned patterns for knitting the "four items most needed in France: a bed sock, an aviator's helmet, hot water bottle cover, and wash rag," no mention was found of the hot water bottle cover or wash rag in local archival materials or the *Arkansas Gazette*.

114 Clarke, 139.

115 "To Rush Knitting for the Soldiers," *Arkansas Gazette*, August 26, 1917.

116 "Red Cross Workers Are Doing Big Bit," *Arkansas Gazette*, October 28, 1917.

117 "Local Red Cross Has Rush Order," *Arkansas Gazette*, December 5, 1917.

118 Report of the Arkansas Woman's Committee, "Reports of County Councils," ASA/LR.

119 "Woman 88 Years Old Works for Red Cross," *Arkansas Gazette*, September 23, 1917.

120 Clarke, 143.

121 Report of the Arkansas Woman's Committee, "Reports of County Councils," ASA/LR.

122 Ibid.

123 Ibid.

124 Ibid.

125 "To Give Sweaters to All Guardsmen," *Arkansas Gazette*, November 4, 1917; "Many Women are Knitting Sweaters," *Arkansas Gazette*, November 9, 1917; "Send Postcards with the Soldiers' Sweaters," *Arkansas Gazette*, November 23, 1917; Report of the Arkansas Woman's Committee, 69, ASA/LR.

126 Ibid.

127 "Knitted Articles for the U.S. Navy," *Arkansas Gazette*, July 1, 1917.

128 Report of the Arkansas Woman's Committee, 64–65, ASA/LR.

129 Ibid.; "Making Comfort Bags for the Battleship Arkansas," *Arkansas Gazette*, August 26, 1917.

130 "Provides for Forty-Three French Children," *Arkansas Gazette*, November 24, 1917.

131 "Fatherless Children of France Society Secures a Number of Contributors during the War," *Arkansas Gazette*, March 24, 1918.

132 Report of the Arkansas Woman's Committee, "Reports of County Councils," ASA/LR.

133 Report of the Arkansas Woman's Committee, 66, ASA/LR.

134 Ibid.

135 Ibid.

136 "Making Comfort Bags for the Battleship Arkansas," *Arkansas Gazette*, August 26, 1917.

137 "Knitted Articles for the U.S. Navy," *Arkansas Gazette*, July 1, 1917.

138 Ibid.

139 Ibid.

140 Ibid.

141 Ibid.

142 Report of the Arkansas Woman's Committee, 16–17, ASA/LR.

143 "Help Wanted–Female," Arkansas Gazette, March 5, 1917.

144 "Help Wanted–Female," *Arkansas Gazette*, December 24, 1917; Ibid., June 5, 1917; Ibid., December 24, 1917.

145 "Girls Work in Bloomers; More Safe and Sanitary than Skirts," *Arkansas Gazette*, January 17, 1917.

146 "Never So Much Work for Women as Now; Those Working for Wedding Rings Barred," *Arkansas Gazette*, October 10, 1917. (The gist of the article was that women must have increased initiative to compete.)

147 "War Work Is Teaching Women the True Worth of Their World's Work," *Arkansas Gazette*, December 21, 1917. (The writer of the article opined that as women enter the workforce, they acquire new happiness and dignity—they're better dressed, healthier, and have a new outlook on life, and they will never give up their jobs.)

148 "Women Working in State's Sawmills," *Arkansas Gazette*, August 1, 1917.

149 Ibid.

150 Ibid.

151 Philip S. Foner, *Women and the American Labor Movement: From Colonial Times to the Eve of World War I* (New York: The Free Press, a Division of MacMillan Publishing, Inc., 1979), 171.

152 Carl N. Degler, *At Odds: Women and the Family in America from the Revolution to the Present* (New York: Oxford University Press, 1980), 402.

153 Report of the Arkansas Woman's Committee, 16, ASA/LR.

154 Ibid.

155 Degler, 155.

156 Report of the Arkansas Woman's Committee, 16–17, ASA/LR.

157 Ibid.

158 Dana Goldstein, *The Teacher Wars: A History of America's Most Embattled Profession* (New York: Doubleday, 2014), 25.

159 "Quit When Women Workers Appear," *Arkansas Gazette*, September 21, 1917.

160 Philip S. Foner, *Women and the American Labor Movement: From World War I to the Present* (New York: The Free Press, a Division of MacMillan Publishing, Inc., 1980): 23–24.

161 "Women Conductors on the Cars Soon," *Arkansas Gazette*, January 9, 1918.

162 Ibid.

163 "No Honest Work Is Derogatory to Woman" (paid advertisement by the Little Rock Railway and Electric Company), *Arkansas Gazette*, January 11, 1918.

164 Ibid. For examples of newspaper articles or pictures touting European women's contributions to the war effort, see "Women Serve Behind Lines: Britain's Experiment Proves Efficiency of Female Workers," *Arkansas Gazette*, September 16, 1917; photograph with caption, "Russian women who took part in a fight to the death with the Germans with bayonets," *Arkansas Gazette*, November 9, 1917; and photograph with caption, "Russian woman sailors who have volunteered to replace the cowardly socialists who deserted," *Arkansas Gazette*, December 2, 1917.

165 Degler, 398.

166 Ibid., 398–99.

167 "A Statement from Discharged Telephone Operators," *Arkansas Gazette*, October 7, 1917.

168 Ibid.

169 "A Statement of Facts to the Public," *Arkansas Gazette*, October 11, 1917.

170 "Ft. Smith Strike Finally Settled," *Arkansas Gazette*, December 27, 1917.

171 Ibid.

172 Foner, *From World War I to the Present*, 91.

173 Foner, *From Colonial Times to the Eve of World War I*, 467.

174 Ibid.

175 Ibid.

176 Steven Mintz, *The Prime of Life: A History of Modern Adulthood* (Cambridge, MA: The Belknap Press of Harvard University Press, 2015), 280–83.

177 "Young Woman Appointed Secretary to Mayor," *Arkansas Gazette*, August 2, 1918; "Woman Made Secretary," *Arkansas Gazette*, August 13, 1918.

178 Report of the Arkansas Woman's Committee. "Reports of County Councils," ASA/LR.

179 "Message from the A.F.W.C. President," *Arkansas Gazette*, January 20, 1918.

180 "Declares Women Should Wake Up," *Arkansas Gazette*, January 20, 1918.

181 Ibid.

182 Ibid.

183 "Registrars to Be Given Quiz Today," *Arkansas Gazette*, February 2, 1918.

184 "Women to Register for War Service," *Arkansas Gazette*, January 6, 1918. (Under the subtitle "To Placard State," the number of posters was, indeed, printed as 75,000.)

185 Unnumbered archival material: completed and signed registration-for-service cards from Crawford County, ASA/LR.

186 Ibid.

187 "Message from the A.F.W.C. President," *Arkansas Gazette,* January 20, 1918.

188 Report of the Arkansas Woman's Committee, 9, ASA/LR.

189 Report of the Arkansas Woman's Committee, "Reports of County Councils," ASA/LR.

190 Ibid.

191 Ibid.

192 Ibid.

193 Shirley Schuette, "Intolerance on the Home Front: Anti-German and Anti-Black Sentiment during the War Years and Beyond," in Michael D. Polston and Guy Lancaster, eds., *To Can the Kaiser: Arkansas and the Great War* (Little Rock: Butler Center Books, 2015), 115.

194 Report of the Arkansas Woman's Committee. "Reports of County Councils," ASA/LR.

195 Ibid.

196 Ibid.

197 Ibid.

198 Ibid.

199 Ibid.

200 J. Blake Perkins, "Persuading Arkansas for War: Propaganda and Homefront Mobilization during the First World War," in Polston and Lancaster, eds., *To Can the Kaiser,* 52.

201 Report of the Arkansas Woman's Committee, "Reports from County Councils," ASA/LR.

202 Report of the Arkansas Woman's Committee, 9, ASA/LR.

203 Ibid.

204 Statistical Abstract of the United States for each year that is included in the chart. http://www.census.gov/library/publications/time-series/statistical_abstracts.html (individual years accessed during the period February through April 2016).

205 Goldstein, 18.

206 Ibid., 27.

207 Ibid.

208 Ibid.

209 Ibid.

210 Ibid., 43.

211 Ibid.

212 Ibid.; see graph above titled "Arkansas's Teachers, 1872 through 1910."

213 Carl H. Moneyhon, *Arkansas and the New South 1874–1919* (Fayetteville: University of Arkansas Press, 1997), 127; Calvin R. Ledbetter Jr., *Carpenter from Conway: George Washington Donaghey as Governor of Arkansas 1909–1913* (Fayetteville: University of Arkansas

Press, 1993), 12. (For an insightful biographical account of one pupil's experience in the Arkansas Delta during the late nineteenth century, see the early chapters of AnnieLaura M. Jaggers, *A Nude Singularity: Lily Peter of Arkansas* (Conway: University of Central Arkansas Press, 1993).

214 Report of the Arkansas Woman's Committee, "Reports of County Councils," ASA/LR.

215 Ibid.

216 Ibid.

217 Statistical Abstract of the United States.

218 Goldstein, 4.

219 "Searcy Girls to Drill," *Arkansas Gazette*, June 10, 1917.

220 "Training Camp for Women at Hardy," *Arkansas Gazette*, June 11, 1917.

221 "Army Wants Nurses," *Arkansas Gazette*, November 30, 1917.

222 Report of the Arkansas Woman's Committee, 16, ASA/LR.

223 "Nurses Likely to Be in Demand," *Arkansas Gazette*, December 30, 1917.

224 Report of the Arkansas Woman's Committee, "Reports of County Councils," ASA/LR.

225 Ibid.

226 Ibid.

227 Foner, *From World War I to the Present*, 420.

228 Ibid.

229 Ibid.; Elissa Lane Miller, "Arkansas Nurses, 1895 to 1920: A Profile," *Arkansas Historical Quarterly* 47, no. 2 (Summer 1988): 154.

230 "Nurse Examinations," *Arkansas Gazette*, September 30, 1917.

231 "Trained Nurses to Charge $5 a Day," *Arkansas Gazette*, October 6, 1917; "Miss Hutchinson Head of Nurses," *Arkansas Gazette*, October 5, 1917.

232 Miller, 155–56.

233 World War I discharge certificates for 115 Arkansas nurses. Microfilm roll. ASA/LR.

234 Ibid.

235 Ibid.

236 Degler, 281.

237 "Women Organize to Save Food," *Arkansas Gazette*, July 8, 1917.

238 Clarke, 93.

239 Ibid., 94.

240 Ibid., 254.

241 Dorothy Schneider and Carl J. Schneider, *American Women in the Progressive Era, 1900–1920* (New York: Facts on File, 1993), 141.

242 Ibid., 221. For a discussion of efforts by the Arkansas Council of Defense to combat venereal disease among soldiers stationed at Camp Pike, see Gerald Senn, "'Molders of Thought, Directors of Action': The Arkansas Council of Defense, 1917–1918," *Arkansas Historical Quarterly* 36, no. 3 (Autumn 1977): 280–90.

243 "Says Recreation Helps Make Army," *Arkansas Gazette*, June 2, 1917.

244 Ibid.

245 Argenta later became North Little Rock, Arkansas, and Levy became part of North Little Rock.

246 "Society to Help Amuse Soldiers," *Arkansas Gazette*, June 1, 1917.

247 Clarke, 85–86.

248 Ibid.

249 "Ask Republication of This Editorial," *Arkansas Gazette*, August 19, 1917.

250 "Women Organize to Protect Girls," *Arkansas Gazette*, September 20, 1917.

251 Ibid.

252 Ibid.

253 Ibid.

254 Ibid.

255 Clarke, 90.

256 Degler, 281.

257 Ibid.

258 Ibid., 282.

259 Ibid.

260 Elizabeth Griffin Hill, "'A Service That Could Not Be Purchased': Arkansas's Mobilized Womanhood," in Polston and Lancaster, eds., *To*

Can the Kaiser, 99.

261 "General Secretary's Report," *Y.W.C.A. News*, December 26, 1917, Y.W.C.A. (Little Rock) Papers, 1911–1990, CAHC.

262 Ibid.

263 Ibid.

264 Ibid.; "Traveler's Aid Secretary's Report for Year 1917," Y.W.C.A. News, December 26, 1917, CAHC.

265 Cherisse Jones-Branch, "Young Women's Christian Association (YWCA)," Encyclopedia of Arkansas History & Culture, http://www.encyclopediaofarkansas.net/encyclopedia/entry-detail.aspx?entry-ID=4483 (accessed November 10, 2016).

266 "Y.W.C.A. to Establish Hostess House at Camp Pike," *Y.W.C.A. News*, September 26, 1917. Y.W.C.A. (Little Rock) Papers, 1911–1990, CAHC.

267 "Y.W.C.A. Hostess House Opened," *Y.W.C.A. News,* Y.W.C.A. (Little Rock) Papers, 1911–1990, CAHC. Clarke reported that nationwide the Hostess Houses were under the authority of the subcommittee on Proper Chaperonage of Girls.

268 Ibid. (without the comment)

269 Dewey W. Grantham. *Southern Progressivism: The Reconciliation of Progress and Tradition* (Knoxville: University of Tennessee Press, 1983), 23–24. In his study of southern Progressivism, Grantham found that during the early years of the century, southern YWCA directors were important contributors to the Progressive movement in the region as they offered women the opportunity to invoke "the spirit of nobless[e] oblige and Christian compassion" within the club setting to complement the Christian social work they were practicing through their churches.

270 "Annual Report of Employment Department," *Y.W.C.A. News*, December 26, 1917. Y.W.C.A. (Little Rock) Papers, 1911–1990, CAHC.

271 Clarke, 75 (quoting Julia Lathrop).

272 "Defines Relation of Two Governmental Organizations," *Arkansas Gazette*, August 12, 1917.

273 Clarke, 74.

274 Ibid., 74–75; Schneider, 2–8.

275 Clarke, 75 (quoting Julia Lathrop).

276 Report of the Arkansas Woman's Committee, 12–13, ASA/LR.

277 Frances Mitchell Ross, 337. Historians have noted that contests of this sort may have reflected influence of the eugenics movement,

which was a common lecture topic at women's club meetings during the early twentieth century.

278 To combat elevated mortality rates among mothers and newborns, the Sheppard-Towner Maternity and Infancy Act provided $1 million annually in federal aid (for a five-year period) to state programs for mothers and babies, particularly prenatal and newborn care facilities in rural states. http://history.house.gov/HistoricalHighlight/Detail/36084 (accessed November 10, 2016).

279 Moneyhon, 129.

280 Grantham, 310–11.

281 Ibid.

282 Ibid., 311.

283 Ibid.

284 Report of the Arkansas Woman's Committee, "Reports of County Councils," ASA/LR.

285 Ibid.

286 Ibid.

287 Hill, *A Splendid Piece of Work*, chapter three, "The 1920s: Time of Agricultural Depression," and chapter five, "The Early School Lunch Work."

288 "Child Training a Patriotic Service," *Arkansas Gazette*, August 26, 1917.

289 Moneyhon, 126–28.

290 Frances Mitchell Ross, 338.

291 Ibid.

292 Ibid.

293 Ibid., 341.

294 Grantham, 178.

295 Ibid., 179.

296 Ibid., 191.

297 William G. Ross, "Keating-Owen Act of 1916." Major Acts of Congress, 2004. Encyclopedia.com. http://www.encyclopedia.com/doc/1G2-3407400176.html (accessed November 10, 2016).

298 Ibid.

299 "Child Training a Patriotic Service," *Arkansas Gazette*, August 26, 1917. The cited newspaper article included portions of a letter sent out to the woman's committee of each state's council of defense. The en-

tire letter was found in the Arkansas Council of Defense Records at the ASA/LR, and a copy was printed in Clarke, 77–78.

300 Ibid.

301 Ibid.

302 Ibid.

303 "School Attendance Law," *Arkansas Gazette*, October 28, 1917.

304 "Wage Campaign for School Attendance," *Educational News Bulletin*, published by the Arkansas Department of Education, March 1918 (found in the Arkansas Council of Defense Records, ASA/LR).

305 Ibid. The following statement, found on page 79 in Clarke's 1918 book, supplements the comment concerning Britain's child labor activities during the war: "It cannot but stir American women to know that England, after three years of war, is urging through the Departmental Committee on Education, a new law, keeping children in school until fourteen, allowing no exemptions and including all rural children and thus going far greater lengths than the United States law."

306 "Wage Campaign for School Attendance," *Educational News Bulletin*.

307 Ibid.

308 Ibid.

309 Children's Year Leaflet No. 7, "Back to School Drive: Plan of Organization." (no date or signature.) Folder 360, Arkansas Council of Defense Records, ASA/LR.

310 Memorandum from Dr. Jessica B. Poixette, Chief, Child Conservation Section, Council of National Defense, "Child Welfare Back-to-School Drive," to the State Chairmen of Child Welfare, dated November 13, 1918. Folder 19, Council of Defense, ASA/LR; Children's Year Leaflet No. 7, "Back to School Drive: Plan of Organization" (no date or signature). Folder 360, Arkansas Council of Defense Records, AHA; Children's Year Leaflet No. 8, "Suggestions to Local Committees for the Back-to-School Drive," Folder 19, Arkansas Council of Defense Records, ASA/LR.

311 Report of the Arkansas Woman's Committee, "Report of County Councils," ASA/LR.

312 Ibid.

313 Ibid.

314 Moneyhon, 128.

315 Ibid.

316 Ben F. Johnson, "'All Thoughtful Citizens': The Arkansas School Reform Movement, 1921–1930," *Arkansas Historical Quarterly* 46, no. 2

(Summer 1987): 108, quoting U.S. Bureau of Education, *The Public School System in Arkansas, Part II, Public School Finance,* prepared by Fletcher H. Swift, Bulletin, 1923, No. 11 (Washington, 1923), 8–9. Johnson's essay provides significant—albeit distressing—insight into Arkansas's educational system and Progressive attempts to remedy the situation.

317 Ibid. (footnote 6).

318 "Camp Pike Gazette" (a weekly column), *Arkansas Gazette,* September 26, 1918.

319 "Fort Roots to be Used as Hospital," *Arkansas Gazette,* November 14, 1917. Fort Roots, an army post built around the turn of the century on a cliff above the Arkansas River and across from Little Rock, was used early on in the war as an officer training facility for the National Guard. In November 1917, plans were announced to convert it into a reserve or overflow hospital for the base hospital at Camp Pike.

320 "Jewish Soldiers Guests at Dinner," *Arkansas Gazette,* September 27, 1917.

321 "To Entertain Soldiers," *Arkansas Gazette,* September 20, 1917; "Soldiers' Club Opens Saturday," *Arkansas Gazette,* December 28, 1917.

322 *Arkansas Gazette,* December 22, 1917; "Good Things for Boys in Hospital," *Arkansas Gazette,* December 23, 1917.

323 "Camp Pike Cited for Disease Rate," *Arkansas Gazette,* January 18, 1918; "Higher Sick Rate at Cantonments," *Arkansas Gazette,* January 24, 1918; "Population is Now About 50,000 Men," *Arkansas Gazette,* July 19, 1918; "Influenza Spreads in New England," *Arkansas Gazette,* September 19, 1918.

324 "Camp Pike Gazette," September 26, 1918.

325 "Red Cross to Make Influenza Masks," *Arkansas Gazette,* October 6, 1918.

326 Report of the Arkansas Woman's Committee, 9, ASA/LR.

327 Ibid.; 1918 Annual Narrative Report, State HDA, RG 33, NARA/Fort Worth, Texas.

328 Report of the Arkansas Woman's Committee, "Reports of County Councils," ASA/LR.

329 Ibid.

330 Likely a student military training facility.

331 Report of the Arkansas Woman's Committee, "Reports of County Councils," ASA/LR.

332 Ibid.

333 Ibid.

334 Ibid

335 Ibid.

336 Nancy Hendricks, "Flu Epidemic of 1918," *Encyclopedia of Arkansas History & Culture*, http://encyclopediaofArkansas.net/encyclopedia/entry-detail.aspx?entryID=2229 (accessed November 10, 2016).

337 "Legislature Has Gone into History," *Arkansas Gazette*, March 11, 1917.

338 Janie Synatzske Evins, "Arkansas Women: Their Contribution to Society, Politics, and Business, 1865–1900," *Arkansas Historical Quarterly* 44, no. 2 (Summer 1985): 127.

339 Ibid.

340 Frances Mitchell Ross, 327.

341 Evins, 127.

342 Moneyhon, 118.

343 Ibid.

344 "Woman Suffrage," *Woman's Chronicle*, December 6, 1888, as printed in C. Fred Williams, et al., eds., *A Documentary History of Arkansas* (Fayetteville: University of Arkansas Press, 1984), 150.

345 Ibid., 151.

346 Evins, 128–29.

347 Moneyhon, 118.

348 "Withdraws Equal Suffrage Measure," *Arkansas Gazette*, January 24, 1917.

349 Ibid.

350 "Legislature Has Gone into History," *Arkansas Gazette*, March 11, 1917.

351 Ibid.

352 Ibid.

353 Ibid.

354 "Stop Registration of Women Voters," *Arkansas Gazette*, March 14, 1917; "To Permit Women to Pay Poll Tax," *Arkansas Gazette*, March 18, 1917; "Last Chance for the Suffragists," *Arkansas Gazette*, June 25, 1917.

355 "Six Suffragists Are Sent to Jail," *Arkansas Gazette*, June 28, 1917; "Censure Party's Picketing Tactics," *Arkansas Gazette*, July 22, 1917.

356 Woman Suffrage Wins a Victory in Congress," *Arkansas Gazette*, September 25, 1917.

357 Ibid.; "Arkansas Favorable," *Arkansas Gazette*, September 25, 1917.

358 "President Urges Votes for Women," *Arkansas Gazette*, October 26, 1917.

359 Ibid.

360 "Wright Defeated by Women's Vote," *Arkansas Gazette*, November 14, 1917.

361 Ibid.

362 "Miss Jane Pincus Has Small Crowd," *Arkansas Gazette*, November 11, 1917; "First and Only Congresswoman is the Guest of Little Rock Today," *Arkansas Gazette*, November 26, 1917.

363 "An Appeal to the State Suffragists," *Arkansas Gazette*, December 9, 1917.

364 Ibid.

365 "House Votes for National Suffrage," *Arkansas Gazette*, January 7, 1918.

366 Report of the Arkansas Woman's Committee, "Reports of County Councils," ASA/LR.

367 Ibid.

368 Ibid.

369 "Says Alien Enemy Can Vote in State," *Arkansas Gazette*, March 24, 1918.

370 Ibid.

371 Committees Have Begun Their Work," *Arkansas Gazette*, April 17, 1918.

372 Ibid.

373 "Women of Church Ask Equal Rights," *Arkansas Gazette*, May 4, 1918; "Baptist Women Given Full Rights," *Arkansas Gazette*, May 18, 1918.

374 "President Favors Woman Suffrage," *Arkansas Gazette*, June 14, 1918. The text of the newspaper article explained the circumstances of President Wilson's statement: "When a delegation, headed by Mrs. Carrie Chapman-Catt, president of the National Woman Suffrage Association, and Dr. Anna Howard Shaw, honorary president, called at the White House today, the president read to them a reply to a memo-

rial presented to him from the French Union for Woman Suffrage. The French suffragists asked Mr. Wilson to proclaim the principle of woman suffrage one of the fundamental rights of the future."

375 "Convention Favors Votes for Women," *Arkansas Gazette*, July 14, 1918.

376 "Women to Participate: One Will be Chairman of Texas Democratic State Convention," *Arkansas Gazette*, September 3, 1918; "Proposed Arkansas Constitution Printed in *Arkansas Gazette*," *Arkansas Gazette*, September 21, 1918.

377 "Woman Suffrage Beaten in Senate," *Arkansas Gazette*, October 2, 1918.

378 A. Elizabeth Taylor, "The Woman Suffrage Movement in Arkansas," *Arkansas Historical Quarterly* 15, no. 1 (Spring 1956): 47 (footnote 180).

379 Ibid.; Moneyhon, 124.

380 Taylor, 50.

381 Ibid.

382 Degler, 281.

383 Ibid.

384 C. Calvin Smith, "Diluting an Institution: The Social Impact of World War II on the Arkansas Family," *Arkansas Historical Quarterly* 39 (Spring 1980): 21.

Bibliography

Primary Sources

Arkansas Baptist State Convention, Riley-Hickingbotham Library Archives and Special Collections, Ouachita Baptist University, Arkadelphia, Arkansas.

Arkansas Cooperative Extension Service. Record Group 33. National Archives and Records Administration, Fort Worth, Texas.

Arkansas Gazette, January 1917 through September 1918.

Arkansas Society of the Daughters of the American Revolution. MSS 97-21. Butler Center for Arkansas Studies, Central Arkansas Library System, Little Rock, Arkansas.

Council of Defense Records. Arkansas State Archives, Little Rock, Arkansas.

Federation of Women's Clubs. UALR.MS.0056. Center for Arkansas History and Culture, University of Arkansas at Little Rock.

National Society of Colonial Dames of America, 1899–1999. UALR. MS.0054. Center for Arkansas History and Culture, University of Arkansas at Little Rock, Little Rock, Arkansas.

Report of the Arkansas State Council of Defense, May 22, 1917, to July 1, 1919. Arkansas State Archives, Little Rock, Arkansas.

Report of the Woman's Committee, Council of Defense for Arkansas, July 1, 1917, to December 30, 1918. Arkansas State Archives, Little Rock, Arkansas.

Statistical Abstract of the United States (various years from 1872 to 1924). U.S. Bureau of the Census. http://www.census.gov/library/publications/time-series/statistical_abstracts.html (accessed December 16, 2016).

U.S. Department of Agriculture Circular 109, *Cottage Cheese Dishes*. Government Printing Office, 1918.

World War I Nurses' Discharge Papers, one microfilm roll. Arkansas State Archives, Little Rock, Arkansas.

Y.W.C.A. (Little Rock) Papers. Center for Arkansas History and Culture, University of Arkansas at Little Rock, Little Rock, Arkansas.

Secondary Sources

Cahill, Bernadette. *Arkansas Women and the Right to Vote: The Little Rock Campaigns, 1868–1920*. Little Rock: Butler Center Books, 2015.

Clark, Judith Freeman. *America's Gilded Age: An Eyewitness History.* New York: Facts on File, 1992.

Clarke, Ida Clyde. *American Women and the World War.* New York: D. Appleton and Company, 1918.

D'Antonio, Patricia. *American Nursing: A History of Knowledge, Authority, and the Meaning of Work.* Baltimore, MD: Johns Hopkins University Press, 2010.

Degler, Carl N. *At Odds: Women and the Family in America from the Revolution to the Present.* New York: Oxford University Press, 1980.

Delegard, Kirsten. "Women's Movements, 1880–1890s," in *A Companion to American Women's History,* ed. Nancy A. Hewitt. United Kingdom: Blackwell Publishers, 2002.

Evins, Janie Synatzske. "Arkansas Women: Their Contribution to Society, Politics, and Business, 1865–1900." *Arkansas Historical Quarterly* 44, no. 2 (Summer 1985): 118–33.

Foner, Philip S. *Women and the American Labor Movement: From Colonial Times to the Eve of World War I.* New York: The Free Press, a Division of MacMillan Publishing, Inc., 1979.

———. *Women and the American Labor Movement: From World War I to the Present.* New York: The Free Press, a Division of MacMillan Publishing, Inc., 1980.

Goldstein, Dana. *The Teacher Wars: A History of America's Most Embattled Profession.* New York: Doubleday, 2014.

Grantham, Dewey W. *Southern Progressivism: The Reconciliation of Progress and Tradition.* Knoxville: University of Tennessee Press, 1983.

Hallett, Christine E. *Veiled Warriors: Allied Nurses of the First World War.* Oxford, UK: Oxford University Press, 2014.

Hamman, Anna B. "The Fireless Cooker." *American Journal of Nursing* 10, no. 9 (June 1910).

Harper, Ida Husted. *The Life and Work of Susan B. Anthony.* Vol. 2. Indianapolis: Hollenberg Press, 1898.

Hill, Elizabeth Griffin. "'A Service That Could Not Be Purchased': Arkansas's Mobilized Womanhood." In Michael D. Polston and Guy Lancaster, eds., *To Can the Kaiser: Arkansas and the Great War.* Little Rock: Butler Center Books, 2015.

———. *A Splendid Piece of Work 1912–2012: One Hundred Years of Arkansas's Home Demonstration and Extension Homemakers Clubs.* N.p.: 2012.

Jaggers, AnnieLaura M. *A Nude Singularity: Lily Peter of Arkansas*. Conway: University of Central Arkansas Press, 1993.

Johnson, Ben F. "'All Thoughtful Citizens': The Arkansas School Reform Movement, 1921–1930." *Arkansas Historical Quarterly* 46, no. 2 (Summer 1987): 105–32.

Jones, Dorsey D. "Catherine Campbell Cuningham, Advocate of Equal Rights for Women." *Arkansas Historical Quarterly* 12, no. 2 (Summer 1953): 85–90.

Jones-Branch, Cherisse. "Young Women's Christian Association (YWCA)," Encyclopedia of Arkansas History & Culture. http://www.encyclopediaofarkansas.net/encyclopedia/entry-detail.aspx?entry-ID=4483 (accessed December 16, 2016).

Katzman, David M. *Seven Days a Week: Women and Domestic Service in Industrializing America*. New York: Oxford University Press, 1978.

Knight, Louise W. *Jane Addams: Spirit in Action*. New York: W. W. Norton and Company, 2010.

Ledbetter, Calvin R., Jr. *Carpenter from Conway: George Washington Donaghey as Governor of Arkansas 1909–1913*. Fayetteville: University of Arkansas Press, 1993.

Miller, Elissa Lane. "Arkansas Nurses, 1895 to 1920: A Profile." *Arkansas Historical Quarterly* 47, no. 2 (Summer 1988): 154–71.

Mintz, Steven. *The Prime of Life: A History of Modern Adulthood*. Cambridge, MA: Belknap Press of Harvard University Press, 2015.

Moneyhon, Carl H. *Arkansas and the New South, 1874–1929*. Fayetteville: University of Arkansas Press, 1997.

Painter, Nell Irving. *Standing at Armageddon: The United States, 1877–1919*. New York: W. W. Norton and Company, 1989.

Perkins, J. Blake "Persuading Arkansas for War: Propaganda and Home-front Mobilization during the First World War." In Michael D. Polston and Guy Lancaster, eds., *To Can the Kaiser: Arkansas and the Great War*. Little Rock: Butler Center Books, 2015.

Polston, Michael D., and Guy Lancaster, eds. *To Can the Kaiser: Arkansas and the Great War*. Little Rock: Butler Center Books, 2015.

Ross, Frances Mitchell. "The New Woman as Club Woman and Social Activist in Turn of the Century Arkansas." *Arkansas Historical Quarterly* 50, no. 4 (Winter 1991): 317–51.

Ross, William G. "Keating-Owen Act of 1916." Major Acts of Congress, 2004. Encyclopedia.com. http://www.encyclopedia.com/doc/1G2-3407400176.html (accessed November 10, 2016).

Schlereth, Thomas J. *Victorian America: Transformations in Everyday Life 1876–1915*. New York: HarperPerennial, 1992.

Schneider, Dorothy, and Carl J. Schneider. *American Women in the Progressive Era, 1900–1920*. New York: Facts on File, 1993.

Scholle, Sarah Hudson. *The Pain in Prevention: A History of Public Health in Arkansas*. Little Rock: Arkansas Department of Health, 1990.

Schuette, Shirley. "Intolerance on the Home Front: Anti-German and Anti-Black Sentiment during the War Years and Beyond." In Michael D. Polston and Guy Lancaster, eds., *To Can the Kaiser: Arkansas and the Great War*. Little Rock: Butler Center Books, 2015.

Senn, Gerald. "Molders of Thought, Directors of Action: The Arkansas Council of Defense, 1917–1918." *Arkansas Historical Quarterly* 36, no. 3 (Autumn 1977): 280–90.

Smith, C. Calvin. "Diluting an Institution: The Social Impact of World War II on the Arkansas Family." *Arkansas Historical Quarterly* 39 (Spring 1980).

Smith, Page. *America Enters the World: A People's History of the Progressive Era and World War I*. New York: McGraw-Hill Book Company, 1985.

Taylor, A. Elizabeth. "The Woman Suffrage Movement in Arkansas." *Arkansas Historical Quarterly* 15, no. 1 (Spring 1956): 17–52.

Wertheimer, Barbara Mayer. *We Were There: The Story of Working Women in America*. New York: Pantheon Press, 1977.

Whayne, Jeannie M., et al. *Arkansas: A Narrative History*, 2nd ed. Fayetteville: University of Arkansas Press, 2013.

Williams, C. Fred, et al., eds. *A Documentary History of Arkansas*. Fayetteville: University of Arkansas Press, 1984.

_____. *A Documentary History of Arkansas*. 2nd ed. Fayetteville: University of Arkansas Press, 2013.

Index

[Note: Italicized page numbers denote pages on which a photograph appears.]

Belgium 19, 21
Bennett, Allie R. 86
Benton 86
Blacknall, Helen K. 85
Blytheville 58
Board of Commerce 23, 103
Bonslagel, Connie J. 30-31
Britain 53, 67, 149, 156
Brookings 76
Brooklyn, NY 67
Brough, Anne 13, 17, 102
Brough, Charles H. 13, 16-17, 23, 56, 58, 65, 73, *99*, 100, 128, 136
Brough's Guards 83
Bucilla needles 60
Bureau of the Census 80
Camp Beauregard, Alexandria, LA 56
Camp Pike 69, 86, *94-96*, 100-101, 106, 108, 109, 122-123, 153, 157
cantonment (temporary military quarters) 7, 11, 55, 69, 83, 100-101, 106, 108,
   123, 139
Catholic Church 23
Center Ridge *99*
Chicago, IL 71, 73
Chicot County 22, 76
child labor 14, 81-82, 114-119, 126, 128, 139, 156
children 7, 11, 17, 20, 26, 29, 57-59, 63, 65, 73, 76-78, 81, *99*, 107, 110, 111,
   112-120, 124, 126, 135, 139, 156
Children's Bureau (U.S. Department of Labor) 110-112
Children's Year 111-112, 115
church women's organizations 5, 38, 51, 103, 124
Clark County 124, 126
Clarke, Ida Clyde 53, 55, 110, 147, 154, 156
Clay County 76
Cleveland, OH 67
club women 11, 14, 73, 104, 129, 141
Columbia County 113
comfort bags 57, 59
Commercial Economy Board 29
Commission on Industrial Relations, U.S. 71
Commission on Training Camp Activities, U.S. 100, 102
Constitutional Convention, Arkansas 126, 128, 129, 132, 133, 134
consumers 38, 40, 41
Conway 16, 124
Conway County 55
Conway, May F. 106
cooking 11, 26, 37, 38, 46, 74, 76, 146

Cooperative Extension Service 28, 30, 35, 113, 137, 144
corn sugar 37, 49, 145
Cotnam, Florence B. 131, 133
cottage cheese 26, 31, 33-35, 41-45, 137
Council of Defense for Arkansas 13, 16, 17, 21, 58, *87*, 101-102, 124, 141
Council of Jewish Women 122, 125
Council of National Defense 12, 16, 29, 30, 115, 141
county woman's committees 23, 38, 79
Craighead County 76, 113, 124
cranberries 38
Crawford County 14, 31, 38, 55, 74, 77, 82, 113, 119
Cross County 120
Cuningham, Catherine Campbell 127
Dallas County 58, 78
Dallas, TX 69
Daughters of the American Revolution (DAR) 51, 55, 56, 123
doughboys 101
Drew County 113, 120
economy of scarcity 40
education 11, 13, 17-21, 30, 80-82, 84, 108, 111, 114-115, 117, 120, 128, 135
Educational News Bulletin (Arkansas) 118
employment 11, 63-64, 70, 106, 108-109, 115-116
England, Leonora 102
England, Lloyd 56
eugenics movement 154
Fatherless Children of France 57
Faulkner County 82, 124
Fayetteville 9, 65
Federal Child Labor Law 114, 116, 117, 118
Federation of Colored Women's Clubs 11
First Arkansas Regiment 101, 102
"Flapper" 103
Food/conservation 11-13, 17, 19-23, 25-28, 30-31, 33, 35, 38-39, 77, 79, 113, 137
Fordyce 58
Forrest City 127
Fort Roots 101, 122, 157
Fort Smith 65, 68, 70, 71, 85, *91*, *93*, 127, 130
Fort Smith Crossing in Argenta/North Little Rock 67, *92*
Fort Smith Trades and Labor Council 70
Forty-first General Assembly of the State of Arkansas 128
Fosdick, Raymond B. 100, 102, 103
four-minute speeches 75
France 14, 21, 32, 51-58, 77, 118, 147
Franklin County 120

Social Purity movement 105
South Dakota 120
Southern Baptist Convention annual conference 133-134
Southwestern Bell Telephone Company 68-69, 71, 74, *91*
Springdale 86
St. John's Hospital, Fort Smith 85
St. Louis 54, 69
St. Louis District of Red Cross 54
starve the garbage pail 14
Stewart, Agathe C. 72
Stifft's Jewelers 30, 40
Stone County 28, 39, 76
Stuttgart 127
Success 76
suffrage 12-14, 51, 77, 105, 126-136, 159
surgical dressings 17, 52, 54
take-a-soldier-home-to-dinner campaign 102
teachers 7, 28, 66, 79-82, 113-118, 120, 131, 137-138
telephone operators 68-71, 74-75, *91*
Texarkana 113
Texas 135
Thompson, Mrs. E. G. 58-59
Thompson, Rev. R. B. 101
thrift garden movement 28
Tobin, Monsignor Thomas V. 23
tote-your-own-bundle-campaign 40
Townsend, Wallace 21
travelers' aid matrons 106-107
truancy from school 11, 119
twentieth century 13-14, 155
U.S. Army Medical Corps 17
U.S. Department of Agriculture 19, 30-31, 41
U.S. House of Representatives 130-131
U.S. Senate 132, 134-135
Union County 39
Union Trust Company 28
University of Arkansas *98*, 112, 124
University of Arkansas College of Agriculture 112
USS *Arkansas* 56-57
Van Buren 14, 38, 55, 70, 74, *88*, *90*, *92*, *93*
Van Buren County 76
Vancouver barracks 51, 55
venereal disease 101, 153
Victorian era 13, 139
Wade, Julia 14, 74-75, *93*

About the Author

Elizabeth Griffin Hill grew up in Fort Smith, Arkansas, where she met and married Richard Hill. They moved to North Little Rock in 1964, and she began working at the old VA Hospital on Roosevelt Road. She retired from the Department of Veterans Affairs Medical Center at Fort Roots in 1997 as a personnel management specialist. She earned both her bachelor's and master's degrees from the University of Arkansas at Little Rock (UALR). She is a member of the board of the Arkansas Women's History Institute, and she enjoys honoring our veterans through her membership in the Daughters of the American Revolution. She works with children at Park Hill Baptist Church of North Little Rock, where she is also a choir member. Her daughter, son-in-law, and two grandchildren live nearby, inside Camp Robinson.

While working on her master's in the Department of Rhetoric and Writing at UALR in 2011, Hill was asked to write the story of Arkansas's home demonstration and Extension Homemakers clubs for an upcoming centennial celebration. She and her husband photographed more than 10,000 pages of county agents' narrative reports at the National Archives in Fort Worth, Texas. The result was a 347-page book, *A Splendid Piece of Work*. The experience was life changing for Hill.

During the summer of 2014, Hill conducted extensive primary research in central Arkansas's archives before writing a chapter about the state's women for Butler Center Books' 2015 anthology of essays about World War I, *To Can the Kaiser: Arkansas and the Great War*, edited by Michael D. Polston and Guy Lancaster. Later, she expanded her research into this book, in which she placed the eighteen months of wartime activities within the context of women's history.

CPSIA information can be obtained
at www.ICGtesting.com
Printed in the USA
FSOW01n1933130317
31691FS